Afro-Uruguayan Literature

Afro-Uruguayan Literature

Post-Colonial Perspectives

Marvin A. Lewis

Lewisburg
Bucknell University Press
London: Associated University Presses

Associated University Presses
2010 Eastpark Boulevard
Cranbury, NJ 08512

Associated University Presses
16 Barter Street
London WC1A 2AH, England

Associated University Presses
P.O. Box 338, Port Credit
Mississauga, Ontario
Canada L5G 4L8

The paper used in this publication meets the requirements of the American National Standard for Permanence of Paper for Printed Library Materials Z39.48–1984.

Library of Congress Cataloging-in-Publication Data

Lewis, Marvin A.
    Afro-Uruguayan literature : postcolonial perspectives / Marvin A. Lewis
        p. cm.
    Includes bibliographical references and index.
    ISBN 0-8387-5550-X (alk. paper)
    1. Uruguayan literature—Black authors—History and criticism. 2. Uruguayan literature—20th century—History and criticism. 3. Uruguayan literature—19th century—History and criticism. 4. Blacks—Uruguay—Social life and customs. I. Title

PQ8510.5 .L49 2003
860.9'8960895'0904—dc21

                                                                            2002151127

PRINTED IN THE UNITED STATES OF AMERICA

Contents

Preface

THIS STUDY IS ABOUT REPRESENTATION AND RESISTANCE IN AFRO-Uruguayan culture: *representation* primarily through literary expression in black periodicals, and *resistance* to total domination by the majority Eurocentric culture through popular expression associated with the African heritage. A number of Uruguayan literary historians, primarily Ildefonso Pereda Valdés and Alberto Britos, have written about the contributions of Blacks and included their works in anthologies outside of the national mainstream. Folklorists and sociologists like Rubén Carámbula, Paulo de Carvalho-Neto, Ulises Graceras, Bernardo Kordon, Francisco Merino, Carlos Rama, and others have written about Afro-Uruguayans, but always as a distinct social entity. The types of essentialist approaches employed by these white investigators have been fundamental to our basic awareness of the black experience in Uruguay from slavery to the present.

My purpose is to explore the manner in which Afro-Uruguayans defined, and continue to affirm, their "place" in a country in which societal and self-perceptions were and are constantly shifting. This is a continuing process to which the written record holds the key. It has been common knowledge among literary historians that Afro-Uruguayans published a number of periodicals beginning as early as 1872. It is only now, however, with recent discoveries in the National Library in Montevideo that the extent of this production has become evident. It is primarily through these periodicals, my focus here, that much of the cultural legacy of Afro-Uruguayans can be reconstructed.

My theoretical framwork is "postcolonial" and I apply many of the concepts and ideas outlined by Ashcroft, Griffiths, and Tiffin in their discussion of diverse diasporan populations. I also use the Latin American specific postcolonial considerations, especially those of J. Jorge Klor de Alva, who devises a critical model that is applicable to "U.S. Latinos or Latin American hybrids." Applying the term "hybrids" to people is problematic, but Klor de Alva does make some observations that are pertinent to our study. He states:

> What I propose, then, is that postcoloniality can best be thought of as a form of contestatory/oppositional consciousness, emerging from either preexisting imperial, colonial, or ongoing subaltern conditions, which fosters processes aimed at revising the norms and practices of antecedent or still vital forms of domination. In short, postcoloniality is contained both within colonialism, as a Derridian supplement completing the meaning of this antecedent condition of dependent, asymmetrical relations, *and* outside of it, by its questioning of the very norms that establish the inside/outside, oppressor (colonizer)/oppressed (colonized) binaries that are assumed to characterize the colonial condition.[1]

Relying upon the concepts of Jacques Derrida and Antonio Gramsci, Klor de Alva presents a model that synthesizes the condition of many Latin Americans and especially Afro-Uruguayans. Within the national culture, the attitude of the informed is "contestatory/oppositional" as a result of both "preexisting" *and* ongoing "subaltern conditions." The "inside" and "outside" dichotomy proposed by Klor de Alva is also applicable to Afro-Uruguay, due to the dialectical nature of ethnicity and nationality in that country. Blacks in that country, however, do not perceive of themselves as being "subaltern."

Currently, Afro-Uruguayans are an internally colonized people seeking, for the most part, to become an integral component of mainstream society. This process has been slowed over the years due to discrimination against people phenotypically of African descent. The result of this prejudice and social stratification is the marginalization of black Uruguayans and the exacerbation of their "marginalized" condition. The historical Afro-Uruguayan response has been, and remains, one of resistance to marginalization through cultural expression based "majority" and "minority" models, both "popular" and "learned."

Given the fact that Afro-Uruguayans have Spanish as their means of expression, they have appropriated this vehicle as well as strategies, symbols, and images from mainstream culture to resist the process of being eliminated from the pages of history. Manifestations of black culture, such as the drum culture, dance, music, and heroes like Ansina are essential in the process of creating a sense of ethnic space. The written experience of Afro-Uruguayans is well documented in their newspapers and journals, which provide insight into the degree to which they used national conceptual categories as the source for a re-creation of important aspects of their existence.

This study is, in essence, an exercise in literary history and criticism, since my aim is to reconstruct aspects of the legacy of Afro-Uruguayans who are often not perceived as serious contributors to the cultural evolution of Uruguay. Their omission is evident in any history of Uruguayan literature. Writing about the new forms of literary history, Mario J. Valdés and Linda Hutcheon remark:

> What has come to be called the "literary institution"—the field in which literary experience occurs—is therefore as much a part of this history as is the development of genres of thematic motifs. For this reason, economic, political, and broader cultural and social perspectives on issues like race or gender must be brought to bear in the constructing of any "literary" history today in a different way than they have in the past. Newly theorized by post-colonial and gender theorists, these perspectives help make conscious the ideological underpinnings of the experience of producing and responding to literature—and of writing literary histories.[2]

I do, indeed, bring to bear "economic, political, and broader cultural and social perspectives on issues like race of gender" in this effort to rewrite a significant, but nevertheless forgotten, portion of Uruguayan cultural history. The difference in my approach and that of traditional historians is that the Afro-Uruguayan experiences of "producing and responding to literature" and other aspects of culture are foregrounded.

This study is divided into six chapters. Chapter 1, "Place and Displacement in Afro-Uruguayan Discourse,"analyzes the phenomenon of the creation of a sense of "home," historically, by black Uruguayans. This is a process that has evolved from a physical to a symbolic reality, due to internal displacement caused by history, economics and politics.

Chapter 2, "Periodicals in the Development of Afro-Uruguayan Culture: The Rise and Fall of Black Journalism," discusses the impact of newspapers and magazines upon literary culture and social uplift among Afro-Uruguayans. The contributions of well-known journals such as *La Conservación* (1872) and *Nuestra Raza* (1917) are discussed, alongside newly discovered periodicals like *Acción* (1934), *Renovación* (1939), *Democracia* (1942) and *Rumbo Cierto* (1944). *Mundo Afro* (1988), the newest Afrocentric journal, is also scrutinized. Over the years, black periodicals have been instrumental in redefining the historical role of Ansina, Afro-Uruguayans' only authentic hero. This chapter details the process.

Chapter 3, "Afro-Uruguayan Drum Culture: Comparsa, Carnaval, Candombe," deals with ancestral remnants, cultural affirmation, and the economics of popular culture. Black participation in "Carnaval" as well as the "Desfile de las Llamadas" on February 6 are analyzed within the contexts of cultural syncretism and mainstream appropriation of Afro-Uruguayan traditions.

Chapter 4, "Resistance and Identity in Afro-Uruguayan Poetry," is an exercise in recovery and a thematic evaluation of poems written by black authors from Timoteo Olivera and Marcos Padín in the nineteenth century to Cristina Rodríguez Cabral in the present. There is consistent disaffection with their social circumstances by the writers, expressed literarily through a conflictual relationship with Uruguayan society.

Chapter 5, "Jorge Emilio Cardoso and the Afro-Uruguayan Dramatic Tradition," is a meticulous documentation, through periodical sources, of the evolution of black drama from its imitation of mainstream Uruguayan artists at the beginning of this century to the affirmation of its identity as a vehicle for the expression of Afro-Uruguayans in the present. César Techera, José Isabelino Gares, and Jorge Emilio Cardoso—the leading dramatists—as well as minor playwrights are discussed as outstanding contributors to the genre. This chapter's primary focus, however, is upon the enduring contributions of Cardoso.

Chapter 6, "Richard Piñeyro: The Afro-Uruguayan Writer as Invisible Man," analyzes the writings of a contemporary poet who did not privilege his ethnic identity over the national. Piñeyro is read as a counterdiscourse to the rhetoric of blackness in Afro-Uruguayan poetry. Ethnicity is masked, to a degree, by the author's own existential dilemma of marginality as he struggles to privilege national identity over his personal situation as a black man.

The conclusion summarizes the current status of Afro-Uruguayans and takes a look at what they believe the future holds for them. Questions regarding national and ethnic identity, societal confrontation, and how to fight the prejudice of having no prejudice remain their primary concerns, issues that have historically dominated Afro-Uruguayan written expression. To the extent possible, I include the birth/death dates of the primary authors since most of them are not well known.

Afro-Uruguayan Literature

1

Place and Displacement
in Afro-Uruguayan Discourse

"PLACE AND DISPLACEMENT ARE CRUCIAL FEATURES OF POST-COLONIAL discourse," write the editors of *The Post-Colonial Studies Reader*.[1] They go on to explain that "By 'place' we do not simply mean 'landscape.' Indeed the idea of 'landscape' is predicated upon a particular philosophic tradition in which the objective world is separated from the viewing subject. Rather 'place' in post-colonial societies is a complex interaction of language, history and environment" (391). The editors here are interpreting the postcolonial phenomenon as manifested in the English-speaking experience, but it has implications for other societies. In the case of Spanish-speaking Afro-Uruguay, language is no longer an issue since the tension between Spanish and African languages in the realms of creolization and pidginization no longer exists. The other two issues are foregrounded in the reinterpretation of aspects of history, the creation of Afro-Uruguayan cultural space, and the construction of identity, the focus of this chapter.

The affinity by Afro-Uruguayans for the sections of Montevideo known as the Barrio Sur and Palermo is based more upon cultural ties than the desire to occupy prime real estate. It is in these particular areas that Afro-Uruguayans created their identity and defined and distilled their culture. It is here that the coronation of the Congo kings took place on the sixth of January (Epiphany) and the Candombe originated: where the different Nations maintained their "Salas," or ritual gathering places. These Salas, so important in the creation of a sense of place for the dispossessed Africans, were the most important sites for the maintenance of African culture and its syncretization with the new norms of Uruguay.

Luis Ferreira, Uruguayan ethnomusicologist and cultural historian, lists the location of a number of the Salas of the African nations, either in the Barrio Sur and Palermo, or in their immediate environs. They were: "Los Congos Africanos, Los Benguelas, Los Minas-Magí, Los Minas-Nagó, Los Mozambiques, and La Sala de Lubolos."[2] These were the ancestors of present-day Afro-Uruguayans and this territory is considered, by them, to be their homeland. Although the significance of the ancestral call of the "Llamadas," a celebration and affirmation of black culture through song, dance, and other ritualistic behavior that takes place on the sixth of February, is lost to many in the fervor of Carnaval, knowledgeable Afro-Uruguayans realize the importance of the symbolic appeal of the call for their forebears to be present and participate in the ceremonies.

The physical space that Afro-Uruguayans define as their "homeland" is delineated by Gustavo Goldman, ethnomusicologist, according to the following parameters: "Actualmente limitado por las calles Rambla República Argentina, Ejido, Canelones y Florida, en la época de la colonia formaba parte de lo que se llamaba el 'ejido' de la cuidad, que era la faja de tierra 'de mar a mar ancho' comprendida entre los portones de la ciudadela y una línea a distancia de 'tiro de cañon'"[3] ["Presently bordered by the streets Rambla República Argentina, Ejido, Canelones and Florida, in the Colonial era it formed a part of what was called the 'ejido' of the city, which was the strip of land 'from sea to broad sea,' between the entrances of the fortified center and a line of sight a cannon shot away"] This is where most of the present-day cultural acts by Afro-Uruguayans were first generated.

In his analysis of the importance of the Noche de Reyes (Epiphany, 6 January) in Afro-Uruguayan culture, Goldman relies mostly upon what white scholars and the mainstream press has to say about this ritual, and assumes that there is no documentation beyond the late nineteenth and early twentieth centuries. Here, too, the black press holds the key. In an editorial entitled "Sala de Candombe," in the *Revista Uruguay* (1946), the following observations appear: "en la Noche de Reyes, se reunían nuestras familias para gustar de una de las fiestas que más representaban nuestros antepasados, por comprender que esta fiesta o baile, es original de la 'raza negra'"[4] ["on the Night of the Kings our families gathered to enjoy the festivities which best represented our ancestors, by understanding that this party or dance is an original of the 'black race'"]. The Noche de Reyes is a key element in the location of Afro-Uruguayan culture and more careful attention has to be paid to black sources by investigators who wish to interpret this experience.

The historical basis for the most recent displacement of blacks throughout Montevideo is found in what Luis Ferreira labels "el proceso de dispersión barrial violento y doloroso que sufrió la comunidad afrouruguaya en la segunda mitad del siglo XX" ["the violent and painful process of neighborhood dispersion which the Afrouruguayan community suffered in the second half of the twentieth century"]. Ferreira further states:

A fines de 1978, durante la seguna época de la dictadura uruguaya, los conventillos de Reus al Sur, y el "mediomundo" fueron derrumbados con fines comerciales y político-sociales: la dispersión de familias afrouruguayas, de clase "baja" molesta para los intereses del gobierno municipal. El terreno de Reus al Sur, luego de la dictadura, fue transformado progresivamente—por no decir subrepticiamente—en vergonzoso parque de estacionamiento de materiales viales que termina de ocupar todo el predio en 1995; el terreno del "mediomundo" es, hasta hoy, un baldío abandonado.[5]

[Toward the end of 1978 during the second era of the military dictatorship, the tenements of Reus al Sur, and "mediomundo" were torn down for commercial and sociopolitical motives: the dispersion of Afro-Uruguayan families, of the "lower" class a nuisance for the interests of the municipal government. The site of Reus al Sur, during the dictatorship was transformed progressively—not to say surreptitiously—into a shameful parking lot for highway materials which was shut down in 1995; the site of "mediomundo" is, to this day, an abandoned wasteland.]

These were calculated acts of violence against Afro-Uruguayans and their culture. The negative impact is being felt until this day, since the internal displacement of people caused by the destruction of the "conventillos," or urban tenements, still has not been resolved because there was no systematic plan to relocate the residents. This fact has not been lost by black writers, who are forced to re-create artistically positive aspects of culture that they have been deprived of tangibly.

Romero J. Rodríguez, the leader of Mundo Afro, the most important black organization, is more specific in his assessment of the displacement of Afro-Uruguayans: "De los hechos más trascendentales en la vida de la comunidad afrouruguaya fue la expulsión de sus familias de los Barrios Negros de Montevideo en el año 1976, realizada por la dictadura militar que ordenó que los negros desaparecieran del centro de la ciudad"[6] ["One of the most momentous acts in the life of the Afro-Uruguayan community was the expulsion of its families from the black neighborhoods in Montevideo in 1976, carried out by the military dictatorship which ordered that blacks disappear from the city center"]. Although these acts of aggression were devastating to the black community, the people persisted in maintaining vestiges of black culture through collective acts of resistance. The celebration of the Llamadas is such an activity.

"Redoblante" (Nelson Domínguez), the columnist for *El País*, on the day before the 1999 "Desfile de las Llamadas," summarized accurately the spirit of the event in the following manner: "Desde el fondo mismo de la historia, a impulsos de toda la fuerza ritual del ancestro afrouruguayo, el tambor abuelo arrimará ese sonido que define como pocas otras cosas el alma de la gente sencilla, una pauta de identidad colectiva que le gana al paso del tiempo y las generaciones para afincarse en el vértice justo de la emotividad callejera."[7] [From the very depths of history, with the impulses of all the ritual force of Afrouruguayan ancestry, the grandfather drum will emit that sound which defines like few other things the soul of plain folk, an expression of collective identity which is gained through the passage of time and generations in order to take root in the righteous apex of street emotions]. The Llamadas are the most important Afro-Uruguayan ritual in the creation of a sense of place, of linkage between past and present. The invocation of the ancestors in this act of collective identity transcends time and space and operates within the realm of *myth*. Afro-Uruguayans create a symbolic cultural space which they no longer, for the most part, occupy physically, but to which they are inextricably linked spiritually. This is the message which numerous black artists have attempted to convey, from slavery to the present. The Barrio Sur and Palermo, where the "conventillo" is the central focus, are the sites of Afro-Uruguayan culture that poets interpret as essential components of black ritual.

The mythic Afro-Uruguayan homeland, then, is brought to life annually during the "Desfile de las Llamadas" on February 6 through Montevideo's Barrio Sur and Palermo. The Llamadas, or the calling of the African ancestors, is a central event in Carnaval and the single most important Afro-Uruguayan cultural event. This ritual is engrained in the national consciousness and externalized artistically by numerous black writers.

I will analyze briefly the interpretations rendered by four Afro-Uruguayan poets—none of whom has published a single volume due to their marginalized social and economic status—of the idea of place/displacement. They are: Juan Julio Arrascaeta Jr., José Roberto Suárez, Martha Gularte, and José Santos Carlos Barbosa. Juan Julio Arrascaeta—son—(1923–1999) in the poem "Desfile de las Llamadas," exemplifies this tendency to actualize the mythic and immediate pasts, as well as the present:

> Hoy el Sur de la ciudad
> de su letargo despierta
> surgen risas y murmullos
> de cada ventana abierta;
> mientras tanto por sus calles
> pasea rauda la alegría;
> le dará abrigo la noche
> y se alejará de día
>
> Desfile de las Llamadas
> desde Cuareim hasta Ansina
> que se sabe cuando empieza
> pero no cuando termina;
> calesita de los negros
> que toda la noche gira
> desborde de arroyo manso
> fuera de cauce delira
>
> Ritmo brujo que penetra
> sin saber cómo ni cuándo
> magnetismo que a su paso
> a todos va contagiando;
> reliquia de antepasados
> que el negro jamás olvida
> porque en su sangre la trae
> desde que viene a la vida.[8]
>
> [Today the South of the city
> awakens from its lethargy
> smiles and whispers burst
> from each open window;
> meanwhile through the streets
> happiness moves swiftly;
> it will cover the night
> and chase away the day.

Procession of the Llamadas
from Cuareim to Ansina
it is known when it begins
but not when it ends;
carousel of black folks
which turns all night
overflowing from the tame arroyo
outside of its delirious bank

Bewitched rhythm which penetrates
without knowing how or when
magnetism which with each step
contaminates everybody;
relic of forebearers
that the Black never forgets
because it's in their blood
from the moment they are born.]

Two salient characteristics of this ritual are captured by the poetic voice: the festive attitude as well as an awareness of African ethnic origins. The poem conveys a sense of the physical as well as the spiritual presence of Afro-Uruguayans while bridging a temporal and spatial breach.

This infectious, penetrating rhythm captured by the poem, goes to the very core of spectators and participants caught up in the overwhelming power of ritual. The transcendental nature of the Llamadas make them timeless, a "relic of forebearers/that the Black never forgets/because it's in their blood/from the moment they are born." The Llamadas are cultural, not biological as suggested by the poetic voice, and through tradition and practice, externalized during the activities on 6 February. In essence, the Llamadas are the primary manifestation of the creation of Afro-Uruguayan cultural space, which is, in turn, represented concretely in the physical realities of the "conventillos" [tenements] of Barrio Sur and Palermo, in particular, Cuareim, Ansina, and Medio Mundo.

Other poets have been active, too, in this construction of a sense of place in the Uruguayan literary imagination. José Roberto Suárez (1902–1964), Martha Gularte (1919–2002), the aforementioned Juan Julio Arrascaeta, and José Santos Carlos Barbosa (1917–1995) have given in-depth treatment to this subject. An examination of several other poems will demonstrate the extent to which other creative writers have been engaged in the recreation of Afro-Uruguayan symbolic space over the years.

José Roberto Suárez was one of the first Afro-Uruguayan poets to articulate the importance of the "conventillos" in the preservation of black culture. In "Barrio Reus al Sur" the poetic voice exclaims:

> Para ti barrio querido
> mi barrio Reus al Sur,
> estás en mí muy metido
> como en los ojos la luz.
>
> Barrio de los viejos "Congos"
> y de los "Libertadores"
> te tengo muy en lo hondo
> oh! barrio de mis amores.
>
> Con tus casitas iguales
> a manera de colmenas,
> cantan en los carnavales
> tus negros y tus morenas.
>
> Aquí no se sienten penas
> tiene su imperio el tambor
> en la lonja cuando suena
> el dulce borocotó.
>
> Quien te siente como yo
> en carnaval y año nuevo,
> y también el seis de enero
> en esa calle cortita
> que antes fue Particular.[9]

> [For you my beloved neighborhood
> my neighborhood Reus al Sur,
> you are very deep within me
> like light in the eyes.
>
> Neighborhood of the old "Congos"
> and of the "Libertadores"
> I hold you deep within
> Oh! neighborhood of my loves.
>
> With your similar houses
> just like beehives
> your blacks and colored
> sing in carnivals.
>
> Here no pain is felt
> the drum has its empire
> in the wood when the
> sweet "borocotó" sounds.

May you feel like me
during carnival and new year
and also the sixth of January
in this short little street
which before was Particular.]

The poem begins with an apostrophe, an emotional recognition of
the inseparability of poetic voice and created space. In nearly perfect
rhyme, the reader receives a historical synopsis of the evolution of
the barrio, from the supremacy of the African Nations to the present.
It is here that Afro-Uruguayan culture is defined and distilled, specif-
ically that of the drum, the Candombe, and the Llamadas. Indeed,
"home" is a favorite theme, historically, of Afro-Uruguayan discourse.
There is a nostalgic sense of longing for permanence, since the uprooting from Africa: hence the serious treatment given the issue of
"place," manifested in the concrete reality of the "conventillo," by
Afro-Uruguayan writers from their first efforts in the nineteenth century to the present day.

"A Goddess! As before, as always, almost approaching eighty years
old, the legendary Martha Gularte lived fully the joy of another Carnaval procession," reads the caption beneath a stunningly attractive
photograph of Martha Gularte in *El País.*[10] Gularte is a primary exponent of Afro-Uruguayan culture who has immortalized Cuareim and
Ansina—tenements of the Barrio Sur—in the national consciousness. Her poem, "Cuareim y Ansina," interprets in convincing fashion the displacement of Afro-Uruguayans from what they perceive as
their ancestral territory. In addition to being an internationally recognized vedette, Martha Gularte demonstrates a high degree of poetic sensitivity in this selection:

Ese día no jugaron los niños del conventillo.
Está triste Cuareim, y hasta el ambiente más frío.
Los niños preguntaban —¿mañana mamita adónde nos llevarán?
Madres y abuelas lloraban, no se podían conformar. Las vecinas como
siempre se miraban y cuchicheaban si los morenos se van.
El conventillo se muere si esta gente se va.
Y Cuareim se desmoronó.
Las familias se fueron, deambulando por el mundo, por el maldito
    [dinero.

Fueron manos malvadas que derrumbaron mi alero, olvidaron que en
Cuareim, blancos y negros crecieron.
Desalojaron familias y se murieron abuelos.

Tanto apuro ¿para qué?
Y hoy Cuareim es un terreno.
Desalojaron Ansina.
Todo quedó en la nada. La cuna del niño negro que tanto necesitaba.
Porque siempre fue Ansina y Cuareim el gran orgullo del negro, que
en las noches de llamada hacían bailar al pueblo.
Conventillo fuiste el palacio, fuiste la cuna donde nací, pasé mi
infancia junto a otros niños, fui muy feliz.
Jamás pensaba que con el tiempo te iba a perder.
Siempre soñaba
Que allí por siempre
te iba a tener

Surgen entre las sombras
aquellos días.
Días de gran candombe
Qué hermoso fue
Quiero volver a verte mi conventillo
Por escuchar sus lonjas yo esperaré.
Surgen de esos escombros aquellas noches.
Noches de vino y canto, todo se fue.
Quiero volver a verte mi conventillo, por escuchar tus lonjas yo
        [esperaré.

Tengo tristeza y dolor.
Y los morenos por esos caminos andaremos
Yo tomaré mi copa
Y de eso no hablemos más.[11]

[That day the children in the tenement did not play.
Cuareim is sad and even the atmosphere colder.
The children asked—tomorrow mommy, where will they take us?
Mothers and grandmothers cried, they couldn't adjust. The neighbors
as always looked at one another and gossiped about if the blacks are
        going.
The tenement will die if these people go.
And Cuareim fell apart.
The families left, meandering through the world, because of cursed
        money.

They were evil hands that tore down my roof, they forgot that in
Cuareim, whites and blacks grew up.
They dispossessed families and grandparents died.
Such haste for what?
And today Cuareim is a parking lot.
They emptied Ansina.

Everything remained in nothingness. The birthplace of the black
    child who needed it so much.

Because Ansina and Cuareim always were the great pride of the Black,
who on the nights of the Llamadas made the people dance.
Tenement, you were the palace, the cradle where I was born, spent
my childhood together with other children, I was very happy.
I never thought that with time I was going to lose you.
I always dreamed
That there forever
I would have you.

From amongst the shadows
those days emerge.
Days of great candombe
How beautiful it was
I want to see my tenement again
By listening to its drums I will wait
From those embers those nights emerge.
Nights of wine and song, all went away.
I want to see my tenement again, by listening to its drums I will wait.

I am sad and in pain.
And we Blacks will wander those roads
Me, I will drink my wine
And about that let's not talk any more.]

This poem evolved out of the historical context delineated earlier by
Ferreira and Rodríguez. Dislocation and the loss of cultural continuity are the primary motifs of "Cuareim y Ansina." With the destruction of the conventillos, the poetic voice perceives the profound
impact this act will have upon the younger generations of Afro-
Uruguayans. "Where will they take us" reflects the lack of control of
their destiny exercised by the inhabitants, and the inherent sadness
with the situation of impotence. This is, perhaps, the single most de-
structive act in contemporary Afro-Uruguayan history. "Destroy,"
"wanderer," "tear down," and "evict" are the highly charged action
verbs that convey the sense of violence rendered upon the residents
and the destruction and death it caused.

Beyond the emotional level of the meaning of the loss of the conventillo is a deeper significance. Cuareim and Ansina is "This birthplace of the black child who needed it so much." On a more personal
level, "you were the cradle where I was born." The cradle of Afro-
Uruguayan culture has been destroyed, her children are condemned
to perpetual exile; "and black people will wander those roads." The

concrete homelessness occasioned by the military uprooting exacerbates the sense of loss from the African homeland, thereby creating a double estrangement.

The same sense of loss and longing is conveyed by Juan Julio Arrascaeta in "Medio Mundo y Calle Ansina":

> Sentado en la vieja esquina
> se encuentra el tamborilero
> haciendo sonar el parche
> entre sus pies prisionero
>
> Entonando antiguos versos
> repiquetea sin cesar
> a lo lejos le responde
> tan sólo el rumor del mar
>
> En la calle solitaria
> repercute el instrumento
> y se escuchan sus compases
> como si fuera un lamento
>
> Los barrios Sur y Palermo
> silenciosos han quedado
> tamboril y conventillo
> son historias del pasado
>
> Medio Mundo y Calle Ansina
> unidos en el ayer
> el tiempo los ha borrado;
> ya nunca podrán volver.[12]
>
> [Seated on the old corner
> one finds the drummer
> making the leather sound
> a prisoner between his legs
>
> Emitting old verses
> it rings out nonstop
> in the distance the only
> response is the murmur of the sea
>
> In the lonely street
> the instrument reverberates
> and its rhythms are heard
> as if it were a lament
>
> The barrio Sur and Palermo
> have remained silent

> drum and tenement
> are stories of the past
>
> Medio Mundo and Calle Ansina
> unified in the past
> time has erased them;
> now they can never return.]

In tightly composed octosyllabic verses with consonant rhyme in the even verses, the call of the solitary drummer is answered by the sea and the silence of the nonexistent conventillo. In an attempt to summon together the tribe, the ancestral drum with its "ancient verses" becomes a distant memory, along with the conventillos which no longer exist. There is an air of finality to the poem as the poetic voice recognizes that the physical reality cannot be re-created and with the passage of time, memories too will be lost.

"Lavanderas del Medio Mundo" by José Santos Carlos Barbosa is less serious in tone, although it deals with the issues of exploitation and miscegenation:

> Baila mulata
> que se desatan cuando requiebras
> dos cabras locas bajo tu bata.
> ¿Qué la lejía se enfría?
> Deja mulata que ría
> ¿Qué perderás la jornada?
> No es nada
> mulata color de luna
> mazumba cachugán güe.
> Fruto de amor dolorosa
> de la negra enamorada y el blanco
> que amó y se fue.
> Ahí, viaheé, cachugán, güe.
> África ardiente en tus venas
> mata al blanco de tu piel.
>
> Baila mulata
> que los negros son felices.
> Aquí en la orilla del Plata
> nos quiere mejor el blanco
> que en el norte demócrata.
> Sufren los negros
> Cuba y Haití
> y en Puerto Rico
> pero no aquí.

Suenan las lonjas
baila mulata
que se desatan cuando requiebras
dos cabras locas bajo tu bata.[13]

[Dance mulatta
Let loose when you feel
those two crazy tits under your robe.
Has the bleach gone cold?
Let the mulatta smile
Did you lose the day?
it's nothing
mulatta color of the moon
mazumba cachugán güe.
Fruit of a painful love affair
between an enraptured black woman and white man
who loved and left.
Ahí, viaheé, cachugán, güe.
Africa burns in your veins
it kills the whiteness of your skin.

Dance mulatta
the blacks are happy
Here on the bank of the River Plate
the white man likes us better
than in the democratic north.
The blacks suffer in
Cuba and Haiti
and in Puerto Rico
but not here.
The drums sound
dance mulatta
let loose when you feel
those two crazy tits under your robe.]

Undergirded by irony, the entire poem is based upon the false premise that somehow life was less difficult for blacks in Uruguay than in other countries throughout the Americas. "Here on the banks of the River Plate/the white man likes us better than in the democratic north" is the type of false, racist ideology internalized by many Afro-Uruguayans, who believe they are better off there than elsewhere in the Americas. In stereotypical *negrista* fashion, the "mulatta" presented here as a sex object has nothing to fear, since she represents the effort to "better the race." What is at issue here, though, is the reality of the alienation felt by blacks who are not able to face Uruguayan society on their own terms. They are, rather, forced to blend in with the majority.

In sum, poets like Arrascaeta, Suárez, Gularte, and Barbosa are invaluable in the literary construction of an Afro-Uruguayan sense of place. Through their verses, the reader is privileged to witness the zenith and decline of certain cultural traditions that are being re-created daily through memory and performances by writers and artists. In this regard, poets and other exponents of popular culture share a common goal.

For instance, one of the new "comparsas," or performance groups, to appear in the 1999 Desfile de las Llamadas is "C1080." This group, a spinoff from Morenada, takes its name from Cuareim 1080, the street address where Medio Mundo, the conventillo, formerly stood. Regarding this group, "Redoblante" (Nelson Domínguez) the columnist for *El País* writes:

> Su creador y director Waldemar "Cachila" Silva es uno de los hijos del fraterno 'cacique' Juan Angel Silva, de Morenada, agrupación en la que aquél talló hasta el año pasado . . . "C1080" ofreció un espectáculo a todo candombe con lucimiento en particular de su cuerda de tambores y del consagrado escobero Rodolfo 'Colorado' González.[14]

> [Its creator and director, Waldemar "Cachila" Silva is one of the sons of the brotherly 'cacique' Juan Angel Silva, from Morenada, a group with which the the former worked until last year . . . "C1080" offered a spectacle in full Candombe fashion with special brilliance from its drum corps and the acclaimed escobero, Rodolfo 'Colorado' González.]

Naming, in this instance, assures cultural continuity, as the black community constantly regenerates itself. Medio Mundo is etched in the collective memory of Afro-Uruguayans. Through its performance of the Carnaval ritual, C1080 will actualize aspects of culture associated with black historical and geographical space and sense of belonging. In so doing, it externalizes unifying images and symbols of the Afro-Uruguayan cultural intertext. It is through this unique interaction of history and environment that we gain preliminary insights into the dynamics of black existence in a society that has been reluctant to acknowledge its existence.

2

Periodicals in the Development of Afro-Uruguayan Culture: The Rise and Fall of Black Journalism

In *Black Writers in Latin America* (1979), HIS GROUNDBREAKING STUDY of Afro-Hispanic literature, Richard Jackson, the eminent scholar, writes: "Uruguay never had twenty-five black periodicals such as existed at one time in Cuba in the latter half of the nineteenth century, but Uruguay did have black periodicals like *La Conservación* and *La Propaganda* in the nineteenth century and *Ecos del Porvenir, La Verdad, La Vanguardia, Nuestra Raza, Revista Uruguay, Rumbos,* and *Revista Bahia Hulan Jack* in this century."[1] These outlets were important because Afro-Uruguayans were either unwilling or unable to publish their points of view in mainstream journals.

Mundo Afro, which began publishing in 1988, and has gone through several phases, can be added to this list of periodicals interpreting the black experience in Uruguay. Of the titles enumerated above by Richard Jackson, the *Revista Bahia Hulan Jack* (1958), through the efforts of Manuel Villa and Alberto Britos, the former who died in 2001 and the latter deceased in, 1999, published its last number in January 1999.[2] In this issue of the internationally focused *Bahia Hulan Jack,* which paid homage to Villa, Britos writes that the publication holds "todo un récord para esta clase de publicaciones de carácter cultural, social y de lucha por los derechos de los oprimidos y exaltación de los valores de nuestra etnia sin colores ni matices ni nacionalidades" (1) ["all of a record for this type of publication of cultural and social character and in battle for the rights of the oppressed and exaltation of the values of our ethnicity without colors or nuances or nationalities"].

This chapter adds a new dimension to the pioneering work of Jackson by incorporating additional information regarding Afro-Uruguayan journalists, by demonstrating the importance of journals in the development of black writers, and by showing the role of periodicals in resisting invisibility and affirming an Afro-Uruguayan identity through the written word. Periodicals were thus essential in the affirmation of a sense of place as well as the reconstruction of a black cultural legacy.

Nuestra Raza (1917–1948) had the most profound impact on Afro-Uruguayan intellectual life, of the periodicals discussed, by fostering black consciousness and pride, by publishing creative and critical writings, by supporting black political candidates, and by devoting much of its space and energy to black achievements outside of Uruguay, especially in the United States. *Nuestra Raza* was first published in San Carlos in 1917 and subsequently moved to Montevideo in 1933, where it remained until its demise in 1948. *Rumbos,* another Afro-Uruguayan periodical of substantial longevity, appeared first in Rocha in 1938, was published there until 1945, and eventually moved to Montevideo, where it, too, ceased publication in 1948. There are other periodicals that have not been researched or received sufficient critical attention until now.

During recent investigations in the National Library in Montevideo, Caroll Young, a specialist in Afro-Uruguayan literature, and I consulted a number of black periodicals hitherto unknown to the majority of investigators. They include: *Acción, Ansina, Democracia, Pan, Renovación,* and *Rumbo Cierto* and are just as important to Afro-Uruguayan intellectual tradtions as the aforementioned publications.

Acción was published in Melo, during four stages, from October 1934 through October 1952. *Ansina* was a specialty journal devoted to Afro-Uruguay's most cherished hero and appeared annually from May 1939 to May 1942. *Democracia,* from Rocha, was published in three epochs, from May 1942 through June 1946. *Pan* was unique in that it served as the official voice of the Partido Autóctono Negro, publishing nine numbers from April through December 1937. *Renovación* and *Rumbo Cierto* each survived for a year; the former from July 1939 through August 1940 and the latter from November 1944 through August 1945.

Afro-Uruguayan periodicals were certainly aware of themselves and of their historical significance to Uruguayan culture. In an editorial entitled, "Hoy, como ayer," in which they pay homage to their predecessors, the publishers of the *Revista Uruguay*, voice of the Asociación Cultural y Social Uruguay (ACSU), write: "también tenemos otro órgano de publicidad, *Rumbo Cierto* del que tenemos a la vista su segundo ejemplar con nutrido material—serán a no dudarlo esos periódicos, continuadores de las rutas marcadas por sus sucesores *La Propaganda*, en sus dos épocas, *La Verdad* en sus dos épocas, *La Vanguardia y Nuestra Raza*, que tiene el record de estabilidad"[3] ["we also have any organ of publicity, *Rumbo Cierto* of which we have in hand its second number with abundant material—those periodicals will be without a doubt, continuations of the trails marked by their predecessors *La Propaganda*, in its two eras, *La Verdad* in its two eras, *La Vanguardia* and *Nuestra Raza*, which holds the record for stability"].

From *La Conservación* (1872), the first known black newspaper published in Uruguay, to *Mundo Afro*, the contemporary journal, the message has been one of uplift, of inspiration for the black masses. These publications are important, not only because they provided an outlet for Afro-Uruguayan authors to publish, but they also afforded citizens an opportunity to express their opinions about themselves in a society which often denied them the same rights and privileges as other citizens in the Switzerland of South America.

In fact, Afro-Uruguayan journalism was born on a note of protest against racism. In the inaugural issue of *La Conservación: Organo de la Sociedad de Color*, in an editorial entitled, "Una Ojeada Sobre Nuestra sociedad"/"A Glance at Our Society," the attitude is: "Hagámosles comprender a esos hombres, que aun hoy nos miran en menoscabo que somos tan iguales a ellos, que aunque ostenta nuestra faz un color oscuro, tenemos un corazón que late como el mejor, y abrigamos una misma conciencia."[4] [Let's make them understand, those men who even today look upon us with disdain, that we are their equals even though our faces are a dark color, we have a heart which beats with the best of them and we harbor the same conscience]. Discrimination based upon skin color and equal treatment as humans are the issues. The editors of *La Conservación* managed to publish seventeen numbers with the issue of black/white relations a primary focus. Not only did the editorial writers express dissatisfaction with Uruguayan society, but the creative writers did so as well. *La Conservación*, in its brief existence, was unrelenting in its pursuit of equality and justice for Afro-Uruguayans. The defiant nature of this publication is captured in "A la raza de color"/"To the Colored Race," a poem by Marcos Padín, which was published in the last issue of *La Conservación*.[5]

Levanta ¡oh! Raza tu famosa diestra
Contra el audás y vil usurpador
Que con intrigas viles y cobardes
Nuestros sagrados derechos postergó.

¡Levanta sí! De ese letargo inerte
En que as vivido hasta el presente sol.
No seamos ya la presa del creyente
Reneguemos del vil estafador.

Que en tablas de oro con letras de brillantes
El nombre de los héroes quedará
Que supieron proclamar sus derechos
Y dejar a su raza libertad.

Noble raza ¿quién creyera?
Que tu imagen celestial
Reluciera placentera
Ante la gloria inmortal.

¡Oh! cual bella, sois hoy día
Quien no envidia el porvenir
De ti, raza que en el día
Vas al blanco a combatir.

[Raise up, Oh! Race your famous right hand
Against the bold and vile usurper
Who with vile and cowardly acts
Negated our sacred rights.

Rise up, yes! from that inert lethargy
In which you have lived to the present day.
Let's not be the prize of the believer
Let's distance ourselves from the fraudster.

Let the name of the heroes remain
On a golden board with bright letters
Those who found out how to proclaim their rights
And leave their race free.

Noble race, who would have believed
That your heavenly image
Would beam peacefully
Before immortal glory.

Oh! how beautiful you are today
Who does not envy the future
Of you, race who on the day
You go out to fight the white man.]

As poetry, apostrophe is used to humanize a physically dispossessed, culturally estranged, and legally jettisoned people. The message contained in the editorials and most of the poems published in *La Conservación* is that only through resistance to white domination will Afro-Uruguayans make progress in the society. *La Conservación* subsequently served as a model for other black periodicals in foregrounding crucial issues regarding color, class, and ethnicity. The intensity with which these concerns was addressed differed from publication to publication. *Nuestra Raza* and *Rumbos,* two of the longer standing Afro-Uruguayan periodicals, professed black unity as their primary objective, rather than rebellion of retribution.

In the first number of *Nuestra Raza: de la raza, por la raza y para la raza* (1917), the editorial states: "Al venir al estadío de la prensa le hemos hecho animados del mejor propósito, de bregar tesoneramente por los intereses de la raza de color, y por la unión, hoy más necesaria que nunca, de nuestros buenos hermanos"[6] ["Upon arriving at this state in the press we have done so enthused by the best objective, fighting diligently for the interests of the colored race, and for the union, today more necessary than ever, of our good brothers and sisters".] Throughout its long history, *Nuestra Raza* was not as vociferous in its condemnation of Uruguayan racism as *La Conservación,* for example; rather, its editors sought to unify the black collectivity. The mission of *Rumbos: Periódico Independiente de la Raza de Color* was similar. In its first issue the editors proclaimed: "*Rumbos* se inicia en la vida periodística con un solo anhelo: la Unión de Nuestra Raza y pronta realización de un Centro Social que exponga el nivel de cultura de la raza de color en Rocha"[7] ["*Rumbos* begins its periodistic life with a single objective: the Union of Our Race and the prompt achievement of a social center which will exhibit the level of culture of the colored race in Rocha".] Although *Rumbos* first appeared two decades after *Nuestra Raza,* their approach to ethnic relations were similar; the responsibility for improving the plight of Afro-Uruguayans resided with them and not the white majority.

The postures of *La Vanguardia: Organo Defensor de los Intereses de la Raza Negra* and *Acción* are a bit different. *La Vanguardia* seems to have taken a page from *La Conservación* in its first editorial entitled "De Nuevo en la Brecha"/ "Once Again in the Gap": "En el país somos los últimos en el movimiento social y económico; nada representamos como factor de progreso; vivimos al margen, después de haber sido cooperadores eficientes en el período inicial de la gestación nacional."[8] ["In the country we are the last in the social and economic movement; we represent nothing as a factor for progress; we live at the margin, after having been efficient contributors during the initial period of national formation"]. The tone of *Acción* is similar: "es la primera vez que la colectividad de color de este departamento cuenta con un periódico que entrará a bregar por los intereses y derechos de la raza"[9] ["it is the first time that the colored collectivity in this department can count on a periodical which will begin to fight for the interests and rights of the race"]. Historically, Afro-Uruguayan periodicals have taken two basic approaches to their societal concerns. *La Conservación* and *Acción* assumed a more aggressive posture to gain equality while others were less forceful. But in the final analysis, neither aggression nor passivity improved markedly the status of Afro-Uruguayans, politically or economically.

Black periodicals were much more successful as exponents of black culture. Poetry and the essay were the literary genres that received the majority of exposure in these publications. Theatrical performances, dances, beauty contests, and other social events were the focus of cultural pages. The majority of Afro-Uruguayan writers are known to us today because they first published in the black press. They include José Roberto Cisnero, Carlos Cardozo Ferreira, Virginia Brindis de Salas, José Isabelino Gares, Juan Julio Arrascaeta, and Pilar Barrios.

Barrios (1899–1958), the dean of Afro-Uruguayan letters, was first made known to the public through *La Verdad* (published from 1911–1914), for which María Esperanza Barrios, his sister, served as the correspondent from San Carlos. She writes early in his career: "El joven Pilar E. Barrios recitó una hermosa composición literaria, dedicada a los componentes del centro"[10] ["Young Pilar Barrios recited a beautiful composition dedicated to the constituents of the center"]. Pilar Barrios will be mentioned on numerous occasions in *La Verdad* until the Barrios family began publishing *Nuestra Raza* in 1917. In fact, one of the first published poems by Pilar Barrios, entitled "Noche de Amor," appeared in *La Verdad* in 1912 and was subsequently republished in *Nuestra Raza* in 1917.

Afro-Uruguayan periodicals served as the voice of the black community while they existed. But ironically, it was precisely the people whom the journalists placed at center stage who did not support them. The frustrations experienced by *Nuestra Raza, La Verdad, La Vanguardia,* and *Revista Uruguay* are predictably similar. Upon the first cessation of publication by *Nuestra Raza* in San Carlos during its first phase, Ventura Barrios, the managing editor, surmises:

> Con el presente número, cumple nuestra hoja de publicidad diez
> meses de vida, y al llegar aquí, nos vemos obligados a suspender esta
> labor, en la que pusiéramos corazón y pensamiento en holocausto de
> una raza, que, como negación de sí propia, desgasta sus viriles en-
> ergías en las más perjudicial apatía, en el más doloroso ener-
> vamiento.[11]

> [With the current number, our paper celebrates ten years of life, and
> upon arriving at this point, it is necessary for us to suspend this ef-
> fort, in which we invested heart and thought in the holocaust of a
> race which, as a denial of itself, wastes its virile energy in the most
> prejudicial apathy, in the most painful ignorance.]

In each instance, apathy and the lack of tangible results resulting
from the energy invested is cited. The fact that *Nuestra Raza* was
being published in San Carlos where the black population was much
less than that of Montevideo was not the determining factor in its
demise. Several years earlier, *La Verdad* had ceased publication in the
capital because of a lack of subscribers. In an editorial entitled "La
situación del momento y nuestra hoja"/"The Current Situation and
Our Paper," the readers are told:

> En esta triste emergencia, por nuestra parte no omitiremos esfuerzos
> a fin de continuar aún cuando con las demoras del caso sirviendo a
> nuestros suscriptores . . . Pues de lo contrario, nos veremos precisa-
> dos, con el mayor pesar a suprimir momentáreamente la aparición
> del periódico hasta tanto cambie la situación anormal, por la que
> desgraciadamente atravesamos.[12]

> [In this sad emergency, on our part we will not give up the will to
> continue even when there are delays in serving our subscribers . . .
> While on the contrary it will be necessary for us with great regret to
> suspend momentarily the appearance of the periodical until the ab-
> normal situation changes, which unfortunately we are undergoing.]

The failure of these publications also points to the historic difficulty
of constructing a black identity in Uruguay. In spite of their adverse
social and economic status, Afro-Uruguayans still clung to the hope
of being perceived as Uruguayan, period, in spite of the fact that they
were looked upon as black first and Uruguayan second. Consequently, they learned very little from history or from the attitudes to-

ward racism and discrimination articulated years before in *La Conservación* and constantly reiterated in the black press.

Decades later, *La Vanguardia* and the *Revista Uruguay* suffered a similar fate. In the last issue of the former periodical, there is an empassioned plea to subscribers for support: "A fuerza de sacrificios, amparados bajo el escudo de nuestra voluntad llevando como pendón un grande amor a nuestra raza y un grande optimismo vencer la trágica apatía de nuestro ambiente"[13] [Through great sacrifices, protected beneath the shield of our will carrying as a banner a great love of our race and great optimism to conquer the tragic apathy of our environment"]. *Revista Uruguay*, the official publication of the Asociación Cultural y Social Uruguay, survived for almost four years as the major exponent of Afro-Uruguayan cultural activities. Its ending was less vitriolic and spectacular than its predecessors, but also as the result of economics:

> De conformidad con el informe presentado por la dirección de esta publicación, el Consejo Directivo de A.C.S.U. resolvió en su sesión del 27 de octubre ppdo. suspender las próximas ediciones de *Uruguay*, a fin de proceder a regularizar y reorganizar las distintas secciones de la revista.[14]

> [In agreement with the report presented by the leadership of this publication, the Executive Council of ACSU resolved in its session of this past October 27 to suspend the next editions of *Uruguay* with the intention of normalizing and reorganizing the different sections of the journal.]

This message marked the end of *Revista Uruguay*. Throughout the history of black journalism in Uruguay, periodicals run by Afro-Uruguayans promoting their best interests failed. This was due primarily to the unwillingness of blacks in that country to identify with and support an enterprise that could be construed as not in the national interest or that they believed would further marginalize this segment of the population.

PERIODICALS AND THE CONSTRUCTION OF THE MYTH OF ANSINA

Outweighing their failure as economic enterprises are the valuable contributions made by the Afro-Uruguayan press in the conservation of black culture. Reading these publications makes one contemporaneous with preceding generations of struggle that continue today. One cultural icon who was kept "alive" by the black press is Ansina. Not only was he the subject of a number of editorials and fund-raising efforts but also the raw material for creative writers.

Ansina (1760–1860) is an enigmatic figure for Afro-Uruguayan creative writers, due to the historical inability to create a consistent image of this cultural icon. He has evolved from the loyal slave/servant who vowed to follow José Artigas to the end of the earth, to a new identity of warrior/hero. The editors of *Ansina me llaman y Ansina yo soy,* a publication designed to reinterpret the Ansina legend, refer to him in the following manner:

> Don Joaquín Lenzina, negro, fue fundador de la literatura oriental y padre de la patria vieja. Guitarrero arpista, poeta y payador políglota, gestor de ideas y aconteceres junto a Don José, Andresito y tantos otros en los tiempos de los orígenes.[15]

> [Don Joaquín Lenzina, a black man, was founder of Uruguayan literature and father of the old homeland. Guitarist, poet and multilingual "payador," generator of ideas and deeds next to Don José, Andresito and so many others in the times of origins.]

The historical Ansina is somewhere between these two extremes.

Ansina, Joaquín Lenzina, has evolved into an Afro-Uruguayan myth whose trajectory is inextricably bound to that of José Artigas. Artigas was known in his time as "the Protector of Free People." According to John Crow, the historian:

> By 1815 he had brought all of Uruguay and the neighboring portion of Argentina under his control. A couple of years later the Portuguese came down from the north and captured Montevideo; from that time on the star of the Uruguayan national hero began to decline. In 1820 he was forced to retire from his country to Paraguay, where he spoke bitterly of the leaders at Buenos Aires who were attempting to make of their city "a new imperial Rome."[16]

When Artigas went into exile in Paraguay in 1820, he was accompanied by "los remanentes de la división de Pardos (caballería de lanceros y lanceras), más de 200, que se internaron en Paraguay el 5 de setiembre de 1820 y fueron confinados por Gaspar Rodríguez de Francia en un lugar cercano a Asunción llamado Loma Campamento"[17] ["the remnants of the divison of Pardos/Blacks (cavalry of men and women lancers), more than 200, who entered Paraguay the

5th of September 1820 and were confined by Gaspar Rodríguez de Francia in a place near Asunción called Loma Campamento"]. This locale is known today as "Cambá Cuá," where the descendants of the black soldiers who accompanied Artigas into exile still fight for survival. Mundo Afro, the Uruguayan organization, has been instrumental recently in gaining concessions from the Paraguayan government in support of the Afro-Paraguayans' claims of their ancestral lands but their future is not assured.

The irony of the dilemma of the present-day people of Cambá Cuá was summed up in a 1996 *ABC Weekend* article in which the extent to which their land has been appropriated was discussed, alongside the preparation by the Ballet Cambá Cuá to celebrate the Fiesta a San Baltasar:

> En el salón Libertad del Palacio de López se presentará esta noche, a las 20:00, el Ballet Cambá Cuá, en prosecución del Ciclo Cultural '96, organizado por la presidencia de la República. Más allá del frenético ritmo del tamboril, los pobladores de Loma Campamento de Fernando de la Mora tienen una realidad acuciante. Ellos viven como en una isla, desde que un murallón dividió el predio ocupado por sus ancestros.[18]

> [In the Liberty ballroom of the Palacio de López, there will be presented tonight at 20:00 the Ballet Cambá Cuá, in celebration of the Ciclo Cultural '96, organized by the presidency of the Republic. Way beyond the frenetic rhythm of the drum, the residents of Loma Campamento de Fernando de la Mora have a problematic reality. They live like on an island, since a large wall divided the land occupied by their ancestors.]

The wall that now divides Cambá Cuá is symbolic of the social isolation and the harsh reality still faced by the descendants of Ansina in their search for a symbolic and physical home.

The black press has expressed a constant preoccupation with Ansina's "place" in Uruguayan society. Historically, many attempts have been made (such as the Comité Pro Homenaje a Don Manuel Antonio Ledesma/Pro Homage to Don Manuel Antonio Ledesma Committee) to revindicate Ansina and to give him some of the credit he deserves in forging an Uruguayan national identity.[19]

From its rebirth in Montevideo in 1933 to its demise in 1948, *Nuestra Raza* was a firm advocate for reassessing Ansina's image and making known his historical significance. Ansina's importance for Afro-Uruguayans is summed up in an editorial by "Petronio":

"Ansina" el leal servidor del Protector de los pueblos libres, es un héroe—símbolo de la fidelidad de una raza, que, a todas las latitudes en que fue arrojada, ya sea, como medio de una dura explotación, o como aligamiento, de la formación de una nueva raza, fundidas sobre las aborígenes, ella siempre dio, el más palmario ejemplo de ser sumisa servidor a las ideales de las patrias libertades.[20]

[Ansina, the loyal servant of the protector of free peoples, is a hero—symbol of the loyalty of a race, which, everywhere it was thrown, be it as a means of painful exploitation, or as essence of the formation of a new race, founded upon the indigenous, it always was the most glaring example of being a submissive servant to the ideals of free peoples.]

This attitude is representative of Ansina, the loyal servant, which has been modified as more information regarding his relationship to Artigas became available. During the period 1933–38, Ansina was the historical figure to whom *Nuestra Raza* devoted most of its attention. Black concern for Ansina was, for the most part, ignored by the majority culture, a fact that came to light during the high point of the fight to save his contributions from oblivion. Black journalists were quick to react to any national initiative dealing with Ansina.

Significantly, the editors of *Nuestra Raza* were upset because the black community was not involved in the decision to return Ansina's remains to Uruguay. They write:

Sabemos que ninguna persona ni institución ni la Asociación 'Ansina' cuya fundación data de Diciembre de 1922—aun no disuelta—recibió ninguna comunicación oficial, y muy justificadamente, en el momento de la llegada de los restos de Ansina, su raza que lo siente símbolo de su contribución en la gesta libertadora, estuvo ausente en la tocante ceremonia del reímpatrio.[21]

[We know that neither a single person nor institution nor the Ansina Association whose founding dates to December 1922—still not terminated—received official communication, and justifiably, at the moment of the arrival of the remains of Ansina, his race who views him as a symbol of its contribution to the liberation act, was absent in the corresponding repatriation ceremony.]

In *Nuestra Raza*'s view, the remains of Ansina were symbolically laid to rest in Uruguay on 18 May 1938. Although there is doubt regarding whose ashes are being repatriated, the Uruguayan people "ve en esas

preciadas cenizas traídas al terreño—sean de Ansina, de Montevideo
o de cualquier de los treinta negros que siguieron a Artigas al ex-
ilio—la imagen redivina del sacrificio y abnegación de una raza,
puesta al servicio de la libertad y la Independencia"[22] ["see in those
precious ashes brought to this land—be they of Ansina, of Montevideo or of any of the thirty blacks who followed Ansina into exile—
the image avenges the sacrifice and self-denial of a race, put at the
service of liberty and Independence"]. For many years Manuel Antonio Ledesma was thought to be Ansina, but his identity as Joaquín
Lenzina was finally established.

Due to the fact that they were ignored during the repatriation of
their national hero, the black community finally took matters into its
own hands and established not just another committee, but also a
journal devoted to Ansina matters. *Ansina*, the "Órgano del Comité
Pro-Homenaje a don Manuel Antonio Ledesma," was first published
on 18 May 1939. It was an annual publication that appeared on 18
May 1940, 1941, and 1942. Again, Afro-Uruguayans resorted to the
print medium to document their concerns regarding culture and
representation. Apparently the authors of *Ansina me llaman y Ansina
yo soy* did not have access to this publication because it does not appear as a part of their documentation.

Ansina, as object, is not new to Uruguayan literature and the in-
terpretations are as controversial as the establishment of his identity.
Several poets pay homage to him in the study by Dupuy and Peverini,
Artigas en la poesía de América (1951). Much of the same information is
included in *Ansina me llaman y Ansina yo soy* (1996). One of the early
Uruguayan poets to pay tribute to Ansina in the former study is
Cayetano Silva who, in "Nuestro Fiel Ansina" [Our Loyal Ansina],
writes:

> Artigas, el héroe oriental,
> siempre tuvo a su diestra
> A un hombre fiel y genial
> De una raza la nuestra
> Ansina, fidelísimo
> Compañero a todas horas,
> De la raza de ébano
> Fue un saludo de la aurora.[23]

> [Artigas, the Uruguayan hero
> always had at his right hand
> A loyal and gentle man

> From our race
>   Ansina, very loyal
> A companion at all hours
> Of the black race
> He was a greeting of the dawn.]

In this case, and with most writers who interpret his place in history, Ansina is a mere projection of Artigas. Perhaps one of the most degrading images of Ansina is presented in the poem "Casi todos te olvidaron"/"Almost All Have Forgotten You," by Luisa Luisi, which is intended as a positive interpretation of the historical trajectory of Ansina. Midway through the poem, though, the poetic voice surmises:

> Se dice que tus dientes eran blancos,
> Como negra tu piel.
> Eras como el buen perro ovejero
> Que sirve a su dueño . . .[24]

> [They say your teeth were as white
> As your skin was black.
> You were like a good sheep dog
> Which serves its master . . .]

This stereotypical image of Ansina, both in "Casi todos te olvidaron" and the poems by Cayetano Silva and other writers, has probably done more harm than good to the historical trajectory of Afro-Uruguayans. This image of loyalty, servility, and submissiveness in relation to Uruguayan blacks incarnates social attitudes that they have historically been unable to divest to this day.

It is Afro-Uruguayan creative writers who have undertaken, seriously, the task of reconstructing the image of Afro-Uruguay's most important cultural icon. *Ansina,* the journal, contains a number of poems extolling his virtues. Isidoro Casas Pereyra, the editor, wrote one of the best early poems contextualizing Ansina's trajectory from slavery to myth; published in 1941, it is entitled "Poema a mi abuelo negro"/"Poem to My Black Grandfather":

> El día que saliste maniatado de tus tierras tórridas ¡qué frío!
> El día que saliste de tus tierras tórridas, ya en la bodega del barco
>   ¡qué sudor! ¡Qué cansancio!
> Abuelo negro, en la bodega húmeda, fuiste rimando por primera
>   vez, tu rabia al ritmo de las olas del océano.
> Fuiste manso por fuera y tumultuoso en la entraña . . .

Ah el látigo! . . . Ah el látigo! . . . ¡Qué rebelión gestó en tu espíritu
silvestre!
Menos mal que un día tu pie negro y ancho se posó en América . . .
En esta América que Vigil sueña para todas las razas . . .
Entonces, al grabar nuevas huellas en la tierra, tú, esclavo... Soñaste!
Y se ensanchó en tu pecho soleado, una esperanza . . .
Un día que cayeron las horas en la noche como gotas, tu insomnio
estuvo a punto de cometer un crimen. Soñaste despierto con
matar al patrón que te explotaba . . . Porque tú ya no eras un
hombre. Eras un esclavo! Un esclavo que soñaba como todos
con la plena libertad que no tuviste . . .
¡Has muerto! Pero la savia de tu espíritu, silenciosamente, retoñó en
mí espíritu más nuevo . . .
Y mientras tú estás en la muerte, yo tejo mis ideas alrededor de un
poema para ti.[25]

[The day you left shackled from your scorching lands, how cold!
The day you left your torrid lands, already in the hold of the ship,
what sweat! what fatigue
Black grandfather, in the humid hold, you were rhyming
for the first time, your rage to the rhythm of the ocean's waves.
You were tame on the outside and tumultuous in your gut . . .
Oh the whip! . . . Oh the whip! What resistance it gestated in your
wild spirit!
It's just as well that one day your wide black foot landed
in America . . . In this America which Vigil dreams for all the races . . .
Then, upon recording new trails on the earth, you, a slave . . .
Dreamed! And hope widened in your sunburnt chest . . .
One day as hours fell upon the night like drops, your
insomnia was about to commit a crime. You daydreamed
about killing the master who exploited you. Because
you were no longer a man. You were a slave. A slave
who dreamed like all about the true freedom you did not have.
You have died! But the essence of your spirit,
silently, reappeared in my spirit again . . .
And while you are in death, I weave my ideas around a poem for you.]

"Poema a mi abuelo negro" is broad in scope, capturing symbolically
Ansina's (the Afro-Uruguayan grandfather's) known life history
while encompassing the diaspora experience. "How cold!," "What
sweat!," "What fatigue!" capture effectively the heartless act of imprisonment, the Middle Passage, forced labor, and ultimate fatigue
experienced by Ansina and black people. Apostrophe is effective in
personalizing the experience, which further humanizes this figure,

who represents the origin of black Uruguayans. The unifying images of the poem are those of creativity, dream, and resistance that capture effectively the trauma of imprisonment, the attempt at psychical liberation, and the dream of a better world.

Contemporary Afro-Uruguayan poets, from José Roberto Suárez to Pilar Barrios to Cledia Núñez have sung to Ansina. In fact, it was not the compilers of *Ansina me llaman y Ansina yo soy* who began to put some substance into Ansina's image. José Roberto Suárez began this process in the two poems "Es Así"/"It's This Way," also published in *Nuestra Raza* in 1941, and "Ansina," penned four years later in this same journal. In the former poem, the poetic voice exclaims:

> Basta ya con ufanarnos
> Con fidelidad de Ansina
> El coraje de Falucho y Videla,
> No es así que subiremos a la cima.
> Rebelión grita el espíritu
> y claridad en las conciencias,
> Ya libres de ativismos
> Obremos sin dependencias.[26]

> [Enough boasting
> With the loyalty of Ansina
> The rage of Falucho and Videla,
> It is not this way we will reach the top.
> The spirit shouts rebellion
> and clarity of the consciences
> Now free from stigmas
> Let's work without dependencies.]

In this poem, the so-called "loyal" Ansina is juxtaposed to Falucho and Videla, two warriors of the battle for independence in the River Plate region. The affirmation of the presence of this Afro-Uruguayan myth is even stronger in "Ansina," which was published in the journal, *Rumbo Cierto*:

> Fulge una roja llamarada
> se ilumina nuestro firmamento,
> suena estentórea clarinada,
> marchó Artigas con su regimiento.

> En pos de él también fué "Ansina"
> quién comprendió el sublime ideal,
> demostró también bizarría
> en las cruzadas del pueblo oriental.

El fué jaguar del patrio suelo,
y fué de su raza ardiente crisol
idóneo, puro y abnegado . . .
Fué la confianza del gran Precursor.

Hoy laten nuestros corazones,
su recuerdo vive en nuestra mente,
unió la Historia a dos varones:
Artigas y "Ansina," dos valientes.

El uno, es Padre de la Patria,
el otro, la más pura expresión
del sentir de la Negra Raza,
que dió su vida salvando el honor.[27]

[A red flame surges
it illuminates our sky
sounds a booming bugle call,
Artigas marched with his regiment.

Behind him also went Ansina
who understood the sublime ideal
and also demonstrated daring
in the crusades of the Uruguayan people.

He was a jaguar of the homeland
and he was a flaming matrix of his race
correct, pure and selfless . . .
He was the confidant of the great Precursor.

Today our hearts beat,
his memory lives in our mind,
he unified the history of two men:
Artigas and "Ansina," two warriors.

One is Father of the Nation
the other, the most pure expression
of the feeling of the Black Race,
who gave his life saving its honor.]

Suárez's image of Ansina is that of a warrior, not that of a submissive,
tame follower with no separate identity of his own. Rather than a servant, Ansina is placed on the same bellicose level as Artigas, that is, as
a protagonist of Uruguayan history: "He was a jaguar of the homeland,/a flaming matrix of his race/correct, pure and selfless." This is
not the one-dimensional image of Ansina to which we are accus-
tomed. Instead, the poetic voice presents a complex amalgam of bel-

licosity and civility, characteristics of a true warrior. Most importantly, for Afro-Uruguayans, is the fact that Ansina is presented as a "fiery crucible," symbolic of their origins and representative of a people who acted, rather than merely being acted upon by history.

Pilar Barrios, the great Afro-Uruguayan poet, also sung to Ansina, but in a much more traditional chord than José Roberto Suárez. Barrios's Ansina embodies many of the traditional features associated with the hero, but does not radically alter Ansina's image, as evident in this excerpt from the journal *Acción*:

> característica que se evidencia
> desde los días de nuestro Adán,
> en gesto hermoso, noble y sublime
> es la manera que se define
> la tan vejada raza de Cam.[28]

> [characteristic which is apparent
> from the days of our Adam,
> in a beautiful gesture, noble and sublime
> it is the way that is defined
> the often mistreated race of Ham.]

In this 1946 view, Ansina remains the loyal, noble servant who as a descendant of the Hamites, fulfills his archetypal role, and must bear the burden of blackness. Writing during the same historical period, it is interesting that Suárez and Barrios would have two diametrically opposed views.

Another of the more contemporary interpretations (1960) of Ansina, which builds upon earlier perceptions, is "Evocación de Ansina"/ "Evocation of Ansina," by Cledia Núñez (1906–). Núñez, just as José Roberto Suárez, articulates the essence of what Ansina represented. He is a figure of uplift, imprinted upon the national psyche: Ansina and Artigas represent the two ethnic poles in the constitution of Uruguayan national identity:

> La Patria está de pie frente a sus héroes
> Y Ansina ya está junto al General
> En el recuerdo de los orientales
> Y en la estela que va hacia lo inmortal.
> Ansina no es un mito ni leyenda
> Es raza pura, y más pura la lealtad
> Es pedazo de pueblo en rebeldía
> Que busca, sin descanso, libertad.

Libertad en la gesta de Las Piedras,
Libertad en el éxodo angustioso.
Tremenda soledad en su ostracismo
Y en la Historia su canto más glorioso.
Ejemplo de una raza que perdura
En el recuerdo de la orientalidad.
Duerme su sueño de siglos junto a Artigas.
Sus laureles, sus glorias,
Y un futuro de Patria en Libertad.[29]

[The Homeland is on its feet facing its heroes
And Ansina is now next to the General
In the memory of the Uruguayans
And on the trail which leads to immortality.
Ansina is neither a myth nor legend
He is pure race, and more pure loyalty
He is a segment of the people in rebellion
Who look for, tirelessly, liberty.

Liberty in the deed of Las Piedras,
Liberty in the painful exodus.
Tremendous solitude in its ostracism
And in History its most glorious song.
Example of a race that endures
In the memory of Uruguayans.
He dreams his dream of centuries next to Artigas.
His laurels, his glories,
And a future Homeland in Freedom.]

The images of Ansina and Artigas are inextricably bound in this poem. In this context, however, the poetic voice still manages to create a separate ethnic identity within the national ethos. The primary motif of this poem is "libertad," freedom, which is earned—not granted—as Ansina "Is a segment of the people in rebellion." The poetic voice never subordinated Ansina to Artigas: "And Ansina is next to the General" and "Dreams his dream of centuries next to Artigas." They were partners in a relentless pursuit for freedom and equality.

Due in large part to the efforts of Afro-Uruguayan journalists, Ansina's image has undergone a remarkable transformation from humble servant to a man, a participant in, rather than a victim of, historical circumstances. The image of Ansina is projected by Luisa Luisi, "You were like a good sheepdog/which serves its master,", has been jettisoned by Afro-Uruguayans for a more representative portrayal, as evoked by Suárez and Núñez, for instance. Black people have been successful in re-creating Ansina's image in a manner consistent with the legacy of struggle and resistance endemic to Afro-Uruguayan culture. This process was begun by Isidoro Casas Pereyera in "Poem to My Black Grandfather." The black press, periodicals in this instance, are responsible for rescuing Joaquín Lenzina (Ansina) from the junk heap of history and elevating him to his rightful place as the most revered figure among Uruguayans of African descent.

The responsibility of Afro-Uruguayan periodicals as cultural guardians is far from over, however. In the "Carta del Director"/"Letter from the Director," which inaugurates *Mundo Afro*, the journal, in 1988, Romero Rodríguez states:

> Queremos ser una voz afro-uruguaya, que analice y comunique el pensamiento y el sentir de un componente esencial de nuestra formación nacional. Una voz que exprese los anhelos de la comunidad negra del Uruguay, nuestras vivencias, su particular entonación en el enfoque de la realidad nacional.[30]

> [We want to be an Afro-Uruguayan voice, which analyzes and communicates the thoughts and feelings of an essential component of our national formation. A voice which expresses the desires of the black community of Uruguay, our existence, its particular role in the projection of national reality.]

In this first issue, *Mundo Afro* affirms itself as the primary contemporary journalistic manifestation of Afro-Uruguayan culture. There is a mixture of traditional and modern views of the black experience in that country represented by pioneers such as Manuel Villa, Ildefonso Pereda Valdés, and Alberto Britos, alongside the new generation, which includes Cristina Rodríguez Cabral, Beatriz Santos, and Agapito Carrizo. This number of *Mundo Afro* devotes considerable space to Africa and the United States, while exploring significant issues in the national cultural context. Recurring themes in Afro-Uruguayan culture are articulated here with fresh interpretations: the Candombe, Llamadas, and Barrio Reus al Sur. *Mundo Afro*, no. 1, also contains interviews and poems.

Since its inception, the journal has undergone various transformations—from an independent publication to a supplement of *La República*, a national newspaper, in 1997. Under this format, the publication was able to reach a larger audience, thus reflecting the broader aspirations of the organization's leadership. Año 2, no. 15 (segunda época), 28 June 1998, one of the last numbers, consists of only eight pages devoted primarily to black actors in Hollywood, an interview with the dancer Zulú, the homosexual community, Equatorial Guinea, and soccer.

Revista Mundo Afro has been in hiatus since 1998 and is now in the process of being resurrected. As is apparent in this discussion of the historical evolution of black periodicals in Uruguay, *Mundo Afro*'s fate is symptomatic of the destiny of its predecessors and more than likely of its successors. Afro-Uruguayan periodicals have always been faced with two primary obstacles to their sustainability—audience and money.

In spite of the many ups and downs, however, the legacy of the black press in Uruguay is more positive than negative. The issues raised by *La Conservación* in 1872 are valid concerns today, as evinced in the pages of *Mundo Afro*. Historically, periodicals have struggled but still have had a positive impact upon how Afro-Uruguayans perceived themselves and their society. Even among those at the margins, the pen can be a powerful tool.[31]

3

Afro-Uruguayan Drum Culture: "Comparsa," "Carnaval," "Candombe"

> El Tambor es el alma del Africa Negra, el Tamboril
> en manos del negro es la espiritualidad de su alma.
> [The Drum is the soul of Black Africa, the Drum in the
> hands of the black man is the spirituality of his soul].
> —Juan Julio Arrascaeta Sr.

TAMBOR

THE "COMPARSAS," "CARNAVAL," AND "CANDOMBE" ARE INTEGRAL components of Afro-Uruguayan culture. The Comparsas—ancestral folkloric groups, Carnaval—uninhibited celebration of cultural values, and Candombe—Afro-Uruguayan ritual song/dance—all externalize ritualistic aspects of black culture, which is in various stages of syncretism. As Afro-Uruguayans seek to maintain vestiges of what they consider "lo afro," there is the ongoing pressure from the majority culture to coopt that which is of commercial value and present it to the world packaged as "lo uruguayo."

"Carnaval," "Candombe," through the efforts of the "Comparsas" come together in an impressive show of sights and sounds during January and February when Uruguay is in a festive mood. The inaugural parade for Carnaval 1999, for instance, took place on 29 January along 18 de julio Avenue and was followed on 6 February by the "Desfile de las Llamadas" through the Barrio Sur and Palermo. The subsequent competition to determine the best "comparsas," "murgas," "vedettes," and other performers, lasted well into March. In the midst of this commercial onslaught are many Afro-Uruguayans who are trying to make sense of the evolving cultural norms as they realize

47

that very little of what was once theirs remains. There is little doubt, however, about the "tamboril," a unique Uruguayan version of the drum, and its place in the Afro-Uruguayan mindset, since it is the fundamental instrument in their sacred and profane activities. The above epigraph by Juan Julio Arrascaeta attests to the impassioned attachment of the black population to the symbol.

The relationship between genetics and the drum culture was raised in an interesting exchange between Tomás Olivera Chirimini, Juan Antonio Varese, and "Repique," their informant and protagonist of the book, *Memorias del Tamboril/Memories of the Drum*. The discussion is as follows:

> —¿Sabe m'hijo?—"Repique" se dirigió a mí. Usted nunca podría tocar el tambor como nosotros. Podrá hablar o escribir de él, no lo dudo. Pero nunca podrá tocarlo con la *fuerza* de un negro.
> —Pero hay blancos que lo tocan muy bien. Y hubo famosas "cuerdas" de tambores como "Los esclavos del Nyanza," cuyos integrantes eran casi todos blancos—lo enfrentó Tomás.
> —No es así—retrucó el viejo secamente. Un blanco podrá tocar el tambor con el mismo ritmo, tal vez hasta mejor, pero nunca podrá imprimirle la *fuerza* de un negro . . . ¡Una cosa es el ritmo y otra la *fuerza*![1]

> [—Know something, my son?—Repique addressed me. You would never be able to play the drum like us. You can talk or write about it, no doubt. But you will never be able to play it with the *energy* of a black man.
> —But there are whites who play it very well. And there have been famous drum "ensembles" like "Los Esclavos del Nyanza," whose members were almost all white —Tomás reminded him.
> —That is not the way it is —retorted the old man dryly. A white man will be able to play the drum with the same rhythm, perhaps even better, but he will never be able to transmit to it the *energy* of a black man . . . Rhythm is one thing, *energy* is another.]

The essence of the drum culture is what Afro-Uruguayan creative writers have attempted to capture in their literature for decades. For them the drum is the key element in the construction of an Afro-Uruguayan identity. It is a mythic symbol, a cultural identity marker, with clear linkage to ancestral origins, but with a deeper meaning. Luis Ferreira is correct when he asserts, regarding the drum culture, that "Los Tambores, las Llamadas y las Comparsas de Negros y Lubolos lejos de ser supervivencias son patrimonio cultural y realización colectiva histórica del negro uruguayo, de la comunidad cultural afrouruguaya toda, negra y mestiza, y aspecto fundamental de la herencia cultural uruguaya de base no europea"[2] ["The Drums, the 'Llamadas' and the 'Comparsas'" of Blacks and Lubolos, far from being survivals, are cultural patrimony and collective historical realization of the Uruguayan Black, of all the Afrouruguayan cultural community, black and 'mestizo' and a fundamental aspect of Uruguayan culture of a non-European base"). This attitude is difficult for some Uruguayans to accept since for them, Afro-Uruguayan culture is no different from the national norm into which it has been assimilated. Those Uruguayans of African heritage who acknowledge its positive qualities disagree and share the same understanding of the importance of the Afro-Uruguayan "tamboril" as Luis Ferreira. The drum is a cultural reference that unites Uruguayans and links the African experience worldwide.

In his study of the drum poetry of Aimé Césaire and Nicolás Guillén, Josaphat B. Kubayanda demonstrates how this instrument "serves as myth and metaphor, and as an aesthetic and structural principle."[3] He further states: "I will further indicate how the poets creatively combine poetry, music, and dance, and how they suggestively involve their readers or listeners in appreciating, recreating and redefining various living Africanizing elements in the Caribbean and Latin America" (89). The Afro-Uruguayan drum culture, whether it is manifested in poetry or Candombe, is concerned precisely with how "poetry, music, and dance . . . involve their readers or listeners [and viewers] in appreciating, recreating and redefining various living Africanizing elements" in Uruguay.

The point Repique is trying to make in the aforementioned interview is that the drum "is the king of African musical sensibility and articulation" (Kubayanda, 90). When Repique reiterates that almost anybody can beat a drum but its "fuerza," the essence of its Africanness, is best understood by black people, this is not a racist remark but rather a long-held cultural assumption. After all, acquiring dexterity with this instrument is cultural, not genetic.

Among Afro-Uruguayan poets, Carlos Cardozo Ferreira, José Roberto Suárez, Martha Gularte, Miguel Angel Duarte López, and Juan Julio Arrascaeta Jr. have interpreted best the importance of the drum culture. These writers were not fortunate enough to have a volume of their work published, but, judging from poems that appeared in the black press, several are the equal of Pilar Barrios, the most widely published Afro-Uruguayan author, in terms of depth and sensitivity. Gularte, Duarte López, and Arrascaeta are all contemporary contributors. A brief examination of their poems demonstrates the degree to which their works are informed by the "tamboril."

According to Kubayanda:

> a drum poem refers to a composition suitable for reading aloud, reciting and simultaneously putting to the drumbeat. Because it is intimately related to the drum sound, it creates a powerful rhythmic mood that seems to subordinate the subject matter to the percussion sounds and the music of syllables. The words convey the feel of the music and may contain no direct literal meaning. In other words, in drum poetry language and sound are tied together so unalterably that much is missed through mere silent, meditative reading. The objective of the speaking voice is to explore the realm of sound. (91)

Some, but not all, Afro-Uruguayan drum poetry conforms to this definition. In a diverse group of writers such as these, some of the poems are meant to be set to music, some are meant to be recited aloud, but all are intended to be read and interpreted as works of literary art.

It is useful to begin the analysis with a poem that stresses the intimate relationship between the drum and Afro-Uruguayan culture. In "Del sentir de mi raza"/"Of the Feeling of My Race," Carlos Cardozo Ferreira (b.? d.?), an outstanding Afro-Uruguayan writer of the 1930s and '40s, synthesizes rhythm and state of mind:

> Regamos de ritmos la noche,
> abrazados al tambor;
> tambor que nos dió la ruta
> de los sublimes pruritos;
> Unas cuantas cañitas,
> que las copas llenan de estrellas,
> los parches bien templados . . .
> los corazones ardientes
> por la linfa que nos baña
> —que solo mi raza tienen—
> y ya estamos lanzados
> por la ruta del ensueño.
> Los brazos ya no se cansan
> dando cauce al corazón.
>
> Que en caminos del soñar
> los cansancios se amilanan.
> Raza mía,

tan noble,
¡que el dolor hace cantar
las más dulces canciones!

Me llevaste tu cariño
y solo me quedó la caña,
como un caramelo a un niño.
No me dijiste qué hiciera,
ni qué mal te produjera
al quererte demasiado.[4]

[Let's fill the night with rhythms,
embraced by the drum;
the drum which gave us the direction
of sublime desires:
A few drinks
that the glasses fill with stars,
the drums well tuned . . .
the hearts burning
by the sap that bathes us
—that only my race has —
and we are already launched
along the route of the dream.
The arms are no longer tired of
giving direction to the heart.

Where on the road of dreams
the tired ones are undaunted.
My race,
so noble,
which in pain sings
the sweetest songs!

You took away your love
and only a drink remained,
like candy for a child.
You didn't tell me what to do,
nor what evil befell you
for loving you too much.]

The "tamboril" and black people are inextricably linked as, symbolically, it is portrayed as an object of transition between Africa and America. The playing of the drum is inseparable from that of the beating of the heart as the former is defined as an integral component of Afro-Uruguayan culture. The poem evokes images of the Middle Passage, the strength of black people as well as love and re-

spect for "my race." Ritualistic ceremonial activities associated with
the drum are means of externalizing pain and suffering associated
with oppression in this professing of love of black culture by Cardozo
Ferreira. At the center of the Afro-Uruguayan experience is an instrument that helps the audience in "appreciating, recreating and
defining various living Africanizing elements."

José Roberto Suárez published two poems devoted to the drum
culture. They are "Parche y Madera"/"Leather and Wood" and "Tambor"/"Drum." The latter poem attempts to capture the sound and
sense of this instrument while contextualizing its rhythmic implications:

> La dulce onomatopeya
> de la lonja del tambor
> cuando el palo bate en ella
> nos trae una emoción bella
> que es como fulgor de estrella
> y al hacer la transición
> del sonido a la palabra
> abracadabra
> tambor
> es tu dulce melopeya
> que va diciendo
> tan-gó, tan-gó, tan-gó
> sacudiendo el corazón.
>
> Es entonces que la sangre
> de los negros en alboroto,
> y se nos paran las motas
> y . . . hasta la respiración.
> El alma queda en tensión
> nos electriza la lonja,
> ¿la boca? se nos esponja
> se oscurece la razón
> al sentir el bravo son
> se extravían los sentidos
> al monocorde sonido
> de la augusta majestad
> la que diciendo va,
> tan-gó, tan-gó, tan-gó.
> Tambor
>
> Tambor
> Cuando tú suenas
> hierve la sangre en las venas

y es la fiesta de colores
de los ruidos . . . del olvido . . . /
   ¡y los amores!
Y no hay espíritu abatido
que al sentir, tu emotiva vibración
no sienta la conmoción
de tu isócrona cadencia
la que arrastra a la demencia
de ardiente frenesí
que hoy baila dentro de mí.

   Tambor
   Tambor
Cuando se escucha el compás
de tu ritmo enervador,
no es posible tener paz,
y eres tú, tan tentador
que toda mi alma se inflama
por esa incandescente llama
la que hace que su explosión
desborde mi corazón
cuando tú dices . . .
   Tan-gó
   Tan-gó
   Tan-gó
   Tan-góooo.[5]

[The sweet onomatopeia
of the body of the drum
when the stick strikes it
brings us a beautiful emotion
like the sparkle of a star
and upon making the transition
from sound to word
   abracadabra
   drum
it is your sweet rhythm
which goes
tan-gó, tan-gó, tan-gó
shaking the heart.

It is then that the blood
of the excited blacks,
and our hair stands still
and . . . even our breathing.
The soul remains tense

the drum electrifies us,
the mouth? it gets larger
reason is obscured
upon feeling the brave sound
senses are lost
to the monotonous sound
of the haughty majesty
which is saying,
tan-gó, tan-gó, tan-gó.

Drum
Drum
When you sound
blood boils in the veins
and it is a party of colors
of noise . . . of oblivion . . . /
and of loves!
And there is no broken spirit
which upon feeling, your moving vibration
does not feel the commotion
of your rhythmic cadence
which leads to the dementia
of burning frenzy
which today dances in me.

Drum
Drum
When one hears the beat
of your invigorating rhythm
it is not possible to have peace
and you are so tempting
that my whole soul inflames
for that incandescent flame
which makes your explosion
flood my heart
when you say
Tan-gó
Tan-gó
Tan-gó
Tan-góooo.

From the initial synesthesia to the final onomatopoeic representation, the penetrating nature of the drum is felt in both body and mind. Narrated from a collective Afro-Uruguayan perspective, the impact of the drum upon every fiber of the poetic voice is dramatized as the ancestral call is emitted. The tambor is humanized, a living entity that communicates physically and spiritually. "Leather and Wood" bears the same message, and as drum poems, they create "a powerful rhythmic mood that seems to subordinate the subject matter to the percussion sounds and the music of the syllables."

Martha Gularte is concerned with both origins and presence of the "tamboril" as an ethnic constant in Uruguayan culture as evidenced in the poem, "El Tamborilero"/"The Drummer":

> Te dicen tamborilero
> tamborilero oriental
> tocas con manos de fuego
> ritmo y alma de Senegal.
>
> Todos dicen tamborilero
> sos grande sensacional
> sos la fuerza del candombe
> sos el tambor hecho hombre
> el orgullo del Uruguay
>
> Negro uruguayo africano
> yo he visto sangrar tus manos
> de tanto repiquetear
> negro tambor hecho hombre
> sin tí no habría candombe
> ni tampoco carnaval
>
> Vas avanzando las calles
> con tu loco chás chás chás
> sos el rey de la llamada
> y a tus manos embrujadas
> solo Dios puede parar
>
> Yo te he visto hacer fogatas
> para tus tambores templar
> y así saldrá más sabroso
> tu candombe sin igual
>
> Noche de las llamadas
> encuentro de mil caminos
> donde se entrevera el pueblo
> entre tambores y vino
>
> Todos te aplauden y aclaman
> por tu ritmo y tu compás
> no ven tu lonja mojada
> con tu sangre de inocente
> mientras que baila la gente
> su loca danza de carnaval

Toca tamborilero
suena el candombe febril
y esas manos africanas
le dan vida al tamboril

Te dicen tamborilero
tamborilero oriental
tocas con manos de fuego
ritmo y alma de Senegal.[6]

[They call you drummer
Uruguayan drummer
you play with hands of fire
rhythm and soul of Senegal.

They call you drummer
you are a great sensation
you are the energy of the candombe
you are drum-made man
the pride of Uruguay

Black African Uruguayan
I have seen your hands bleed
from so much playing
black drum-made man
without you there would be no candombe
nor carnaval

You march through the streets
with your crazy chás chás chás
you are king of the llamadas
and your bewitched hands
can only be stopped by God

I have seen you light bonfires
to tune your drums
thus will be more pleasurable
your candombe without equal

Night of the llamadas
meeting of a thousand roads
where the people intermingle
over drums and wine

All applaud and praise you
for your rhythm and your beat
they don't see your drum soaked
with the blood of your innocence

while the people dance
the crazy dance of carnaval

Play drummer
the feverish candombe sounds
and those African hands
give life to the drum

They call you drummer
Uruguayan drummer
you play with hands of fire
rhythm and soul of Senegal.]

This poem locates the drum at the center of Uruguayan Llamadas, Carnaval, and Candombe. The inseparability of human and instrument is again stressed. Fire is the unifying metaphor of this selection as the image of construction of the tamboril is transferred to the hands that relay its penetrating message. The drum as an African cultural identity marker is foregrounded in the location of Afro-Uruguayan roots in Senegal, and subsequently transferred to the Americas with passion and intensity. The poetic voice employs apostrophe to question the extent to which the public understands the profundity of this cultural act.

Miguel Angel Duarte López (1951–) engages in an intimate dialog with the drum which results in a cultural lesson in "Tamboril"/ "Drum":

Tu nombre, me llaman
tamboril, me dicen chico,
porque soy el más pequeño
de mi familia.

Y a mí, me dicen repique
debo de ser el más ruidoso de ellos,
yo soy el piano, medianamente gordito
y mi hermano mayor, el más ronco
de todos, lo llaman el bombo
por su gordura.

Solamente cuatro hermanos
hechos de una misma madera,
moldeados de barrica de yerba,
encadenados por flejes de acero.

Como si fueran nuestras cadenas,
una gorra de cuero de potro

y varias tachuelas, como espinas
clavadas, todas alrededor de mi gorra de potro.

Tensada al máximo, como
si estuviera en un cepo
al sol, esclavizado al igual
que mis hermanos.

Sólo, que mi deseo es que me
terminen, para poder soñar,
junto al resto de mi familia
hecha de madera, fleje, tachuelas
y longa de potro.

Cuando alguien llama, con sus manos
dice chico llama al repique, al piano
y al bombo, que nos vamos a
candombear, allá en el Sur y Palermo.

Donde las llamadas nos
esperan, nuestros padres
primos, tíos, abuelos, mamas
viejas, nietos y bisnietos
de toda una raza.

Hoy es tu día tamboril,
haz que toda esa raza
vibre al son del chico,
repique, piano y bombo.

Salud Hermanos.[7]

[Your name, they call me
drum, they call me "chico"
because I am the smallest
of my family.

Me, they call "repique"
I must be the noisiest of them,
I am the "piano," half fat
and my older brother, the hoarsest
of all, we call him the "bombo"
because of his size.

Only four brothers
made from the same wood,
molded from the trunk of a tree,
chained with bolts of steel.

As if they were our chains
a cap of horse leather
and several nails, like thorns
nailed, around my cap of horse leather.

Stretched to the maximum, as
if it were in a stock in
the sun, enslaved like my brothers.

Only, that my desire is
that you finish me, in order to be able to dream
with the rest of my family
made of wood, metal, nails
and horsehide.

When somebody calls with their hands
they say "chico" calls to "repique,"
"piano," "bombo," that we are going to
do candombe, in Barrio Sur and Palermo.

Where the llamadas await
us, our parents
cousins, uncles, grandparents,
"mamas viejas," grandchildren and great-grandchildren
of a race.

Today is your day drum
make sure all of that race
vibrates to the sound of the "chico,"
"repique," "piano" and "bombo."

Greetings Brothers]

These initial selections by Cardozo Ferreira, Suárez, Gularte, and Duarte López have in common the humanization of the "tamboril" through apostrophe. The poetic "I" in "Tamboril" goes one step further in initially defining the roles of the four basic drums that compose the rhythm section of the Comparsa. In this poem by Duarte López, the connection is made between various generations of Afro-Uruguayans and their historical adherence to the drum culture. The drum, as a prosopopeia, assumes its own voice and creates a series of metaphors related to the bonds of slavery and the fight for freedom. In fact, the images of "wood, metal, nails and horsehair" conjure up the intertextual reference to a slave ship. Just as sounds seek to escape the drum an analogous situation occurred with the African prisoners on board.

Juan Julio Arrascaeta Jr., who died in August 1999, is the contemporary Afro-Uruguayan poet who has devoted the most creative energy to poetry of the drum culture. He dedicates five poems to this theme. They are: "Magia de Tamboril"/"Drum Magic," "Secreto de Tamboril"/"Drum Secret," "Tengo sed de Tamboriles"/"I Thirst for Drums," "Tamboril"/"Drum," and "Tamborilero"/"Drummer." "Tamborilero" captures, in depth, the complexity of the different attitudes toward the drum displayed by Arrascaeta. The poetic voice exclaims:

> Nací entre vivas de lavanderas
> una mañana del mes de abril
> y fue primera canción de cuna
> el suave arrullo de un tamboril
>
> Aprendí luego que es ritmo alegre
> y a veces triste cuando es ritual
> recorrí calles con él a cuestas
> buscando abrigo en algún umbral.
>
> Tamborilero, me llaman todos
> y yo me dejo llamar así
> cuando mis manos baten el parche
> África toda revive en mí.
>
> Es al conjuro de su cadencia
> que yo no puedo tener quietud
> cual la serpiente baila encantada
> por esa flauta del mago hindú
>
> Tamborilero, cuando a tu oído
> llegue el repique que allí a lo lejos
> no sé qué manos baten el parche de tu existir
> de cara al cielo rogad al Supremo
> que nunca muera el tamboril.[8]
>
> [I was born amongst the cheers of washerwomen
> one morning in the month of April
> and the first cradle song was
> the smooth murmur of the drum
>
> I learned right away that it is a happy rhythm
> and at times sad when it is a ritual
> I roamed the streets with it in tow
> seeking shelter in some doorway.
>
> Drummer, they all call me
> and I let it be

when my hands strike the leather
Africa still lives in me.

It is to the conjuring of its cadence
that I cannot rest
like the serpent who dances enchanted
to the flute of the Hindu magician

Drummer, when to your ear
arrives the peal out there in the distance
I don't know which hands strike
the leather of your being
face Heaven pray to the Almighty
that the drum never dies.]

The poem, "Tamborilero," is both an exaltation of the power of the drum and a personal trajectory. Playing this instrument conjures up images of the African past and the spiritual and religious power associated with this act. The personal nature of the drum culture to Afro-Uruguayans is again stressed as the poetic "I" is engaged in reminiscences from childhood to the present. A cultural identity marker, an instrument of resistance to cultural assimilation, the "tamboril" is a constant which Afro-Uruguayans can ill afford to lose. The other selections by Arrascaeta carry variations of the same message regarding the permanence of the drum in Uruguayan culture.

Subsequently, its function is in keeping with drum culture throughout Africa and the diaspora where according to Kubayanda, the drum "is sometimes used in place of the human speaking voice to 'call people or raise an alarm,' to 'give warning, praise or congratulations,' and to produce music for listening and dancing" (92). In Afro-Uruguayan poetry, the Candombe, and the Llamadas, the ancestral drum remains at the center of the cultural traditions of a people marginalized by color but unified in their lasting adherence to tradition.

CANDOMBE

While the Uruguayan Candombe has received a great deal of attention from historians, musicologists, folklorists, sociologists, and other investigators, little attention has been paid to the Candombe as a literary construct of valuable importance to Afro-Uruguayan culture. Recent studies have traced the historical evolution of the Candombe from its nineteenth century origins to its present relationship as an integral component of Carnaval. Abril Trigo, for example, in "Candombe and the Reterritorialization of Culture," approaches this cultural expression from the following perspective:

> Despite the fact that Uruguay is known for its Europeanized culture, the black minority, which constitutes about two percent of the population, has exercised an influence on urban popular culture that greatly exceeds its numbers. *Candombe*, an Afro-Uruguayan rhythm and dance rooted in carnival festivities, has become a main component of Montividean music over the years, and is in fact, one of its foundations. *Candombe*'s continuity, however, was severely jeopardized during the 1970s when the military dictatorship attacked every manifestation of popular culture not adhering to its ideological framework. *Candombe*, once the cultural expression of a minority, then folklorized and duly acculturated by hegemonic society (Certeau, *Heterologies* 124–25), suddenly became politicized; what was once a well-tamed and almost fossilized manifestation of Uruguayan liberalism reterritorialized Uruguayan culture in an unprecedented manner. In its itinerary from the peripheral to center stage, and in the context of a more ample carnivalization of culture, *candombe* developed into a symbol of resistance to neofascism; thus its popularity transcended the boundaries of its minority audience and/or the framework of traditional carnival, to become the foremost representation of Montevidean popular culture.[9]

Trigo is concerned primarily with the music of Candombe and its social implications, and the transition of this art form from margin to Center. Afro-Uruguayans view this process as cultural appropriation. As cultural expression, the Candombe, since its appearance in Uruguay, has always been viewed differently by blacks and whites. This point is made by Isidoro de María, who, in the 19th century, observes:

> Así la buena gente de ese tiempo, encontraba distracción inocente en los candombes y la raza africana entregada alegremente a los usos y recuerdos de Angola, parecía olvidar en aquellos momentos de jolgorio la triste condición del esclavo, y el día en que la codicia y la crueldad de los traficantes lo arrancara de la tierra natal.[10]

> [Thus the good people of that time, found an innocent distraction in the Candombes and the African race engrossed happily in the uses and memories of Angola, seemed to forget in those moments of joy the sad condition of the slave, and the day which the greed and cruelty of the traffickers snatched them from their native soil.]

The dual perception of the Candombe as mere spectacle by whites and as ancestral ritual by blacks is foregrounded in this quote and exemplifies a situation which exists to this day, as a central issue in the commodification of black culture.

According to Lauro Ayestarán, the word "Candombe" first appeared in Uruguayan cultural discourse in the Montevideo daily newspaper, *El Universal*, on 17 November 1834.[11] The attempt to define and categorize "Candombe" continues. For Rubén Carámbula, "El término es genérico para todos los bailes de negros: sinónimo pues, de danza negra, evocación del ritual de la raza. Esta voz, surgió probablemente de la onomatopeya rítmica, característica en los breves cantos afros tan reminiscentes de la selva"[12] ["The term is generic for all dances by blacks: synonymous then, with black dance, evocation of ritual of the race. This word emerged probably from the rhythmic onomatopeia, characteristic of the brief African songs so reminiscent of the jungle"]. Luis Ferreira writes that "Candombe designaba entonces las ocasiones en que los africanos ejecutaban sus danzas nacionales y recreaban, espiritual y simbolicamente, sus sociedades de origen"[13] ["Candombe designated then the occasions on which the Africans executed their national dances and recreated, spiritually and symbolically, their societies of origin"]. The most recent effort to trace the etymology of "Candombe" is by Oscar Montaño, who relies upon Nestor Ortiz Oderigo: "Palabra derivada del prefijo 'ka' de Ndombe (negro), del idioma Kimbundu, rama de las lenguas bantúes que se hablan en el Congo, en Angola y en distintas zonas de Africa del Sur"[14] ["Word derived form the prefix 'ka' of Ndombe (black), of the Kimbundu language, branch of the Bantu languages that are spoken in the Congo, in Angola and in different zones of South Africa"].

In several of the more well-known studies of the Candombe, the differences are more in perspective and interpretation than in breaking new ground. In *El Candombe* (1995), by Rubén Carámbula, an outsider's perspective of the historical evolution of this ritual is presented through documentation, interviews, photographs, reconstruction of lyrics, and choreography. The late Carámbula was both a theorist and practitioner of the art of candombe. Luis Ferreira, in *Los tambores del Candombe* (1997), presents, however, the most profound interpretation of Afro-Uruguayan drum culture available to date. Ferreira, a trained ethnomusicologist, discusses historical antecedents to candombe, Afro-Uruguayan music in general, the significance of the drum in black culture, as well as the dynamics of the beat of various instruments. Reading *Los tambores del Candombe*, one gets the impression that the drum culture is an integral component of Ferreira's upbringing, rather than a learned distance concept. Written in a minor chord is *Las músicas primitivas en el Uruguay* (1997) by Lauro Ayesterán, who devotes a chapter to "La música indígena" and another to "La música negra." The Ayesterán study is outdated, since it was released more than thirty years after his death.

"El Candombe" is the subject of one of the educational *Cuadernillos de Educación Afro/Educational Notebooks*, published by Mundo Afro. In this brief pamphlet of four pages, the historical evolution as well as the mode of presentation of the Candombe as an art form is discussed. The *Cuadernillo* delineates three distinct eras in the evolution of this Afro-Uruguayan ritual. The first, and most authentic, was during slavery, when blacks came together on Sundays to renew African regional and national cultural links; the second was the era of African and European syncretism; while the third is the era of the "comparsas" as we know them today. Of these three stages in the evolution of the Candombe, perhaps the most important in terms of national identity, according to the *Cuadernillo*, is:

> *La segunda etapa* o de las danzas afro-criollas, es precisamente donde se "forma el Candombe," como expresión afro-oriental, se realizó una mezcla entre el baile africano y la contradanza de cuadrilla, y otros elementos coreográficos asimilados del blanco. Este candombe, que se gestó a fines del siglo XVIII y languideció hacia el 1870. (2)

> [The *second phase* or that of the Afro-creole dances is precisely where the Candombe is formed as an Afro-Uruguayan expression, composed of a mixture of African dance and the group counter dance, and other choreographic elements assimilated from the white man. This Candombe, which gestated at the end of the eighteenth century languished around 1870.]

The present-day Candombe, with its comparsas and organizational structure, has evolved for more than a century, as a form of African and European cultural syncretism, according to Mundo Afro.

The "comparsa" or "agrupación lubola," from an Afro-Uruguayan perspective, "es un movimiento social y cultural que tiene como objetivo mantener nuestros conocimientos musicales y religosos que dejaron nuestros antepasados" ["is a social and cultural movement which has as its objective maintaining our musical and religious knowledge left by our ancestors"] (3). The drums are the heart and soul of this cultural tradition: *chico* (soprano); *repique* (contraalto o tenor), and *piano* (tenor o más barítono).

The "comparsa" usually consists of a hundred or more participants, including forty to seventy drummers, the "Mamá Vieja," the "Gramillero," the "Escobero," the "Cuerpo de baile," the "Vedette," the "Bandera," the "Estrellas," and the "Medialuna." The majority of these components is rooted in Afro-Uruguayan cultural heritage. Ironically, it is the Vedette—a scantily clad dancer—perhaps the most popular figure, which is not; "Este personaje se incorporó a las comparsas en los años 50, es actualmente la figura más destacada de la comparsa" ["This personage was incorporated into the procession in the 1950s and is today the most outstanding figure"] (4). Recognizing the fact that the Vedette, more form than substance, is overshadowing traditional figures of the comparsa, Ester Arrascaeta—the most renowned Mamá Vieja of the decade of the 1990s—surmises after the 1999 Desfile de las Llamadas:

"Mamas Viejas hay muy pocas. Es el personaje que menos interesa, pasa lo mismo con los Gramilleros" dijo Ester. "Junto con el Bastonero no pueden morir, porque son los personajes típicos del Carnaval, al igual que la cuerda de tambores. Nosotros decimos que la vedette fue importada de Europa—en tiempos de Josephine Baker— porque en las primeras comparsas solo habían bailarinas."[15]

["There are very few Mama Viejas. It is the figure of least interest, the same thing happens to the Gramilleros," Ester said. "Along with the Bastonero they cannot die, because they are the typical characters of the Carnaval, just like the drum ensembles. We say that the Vedette was imported from Europe—in the times of Josephine Baker—because in the first *comparsas* there were only dancers."]

The outstanding Vedette for 1999, who follows in the footsteps of Martha Gularte and Rosa Luna, Afro-Uruguayans, was Florencia Gularte, "sobrina nieta de la mítica Martha Gularte" [great-niece of the mythic Martha Gularte].

Florencia brings a different perspective from the opinion expressed by Ester Arrascaeta to the situation. This is evident in the same interview:

Muchos sostienen que una buena vedette "requiere cuerpo, movimiento y color." Florencia no está de acuerdo: "Soy blanca y tengo ojos verdes y soy hija de padre negro. Yo no tengo la culpa de ser blanca. Creo que todo eso no tiene mucho sentido . . . cuando me enteré que había ganado el premio, me emocioné porque no lo esperaba. Pensé que iba a tener que tomar mucho sol para que me lo dieran." (5).

[Many maintain that a good vedette "requires body, movement and color." Florencia does not agree. "I am white with green eyes and I am the daughter of a black father. Being white is not my fault. I believe all of that doesn't make sense . . . when I found out that I had won the prize, I became very emotional because I did not expect it. I thought I would have to get a suntan in order for them to give it to me."]

Along with cultural syncretism, miscegenation is a factor in the selection and presentation of female performers in the event. In recent years, the darker-skinned women have been the first to lose out as the judges redefine the Afro-Uruguayan standard of beauty. The further Candombe is away from the black norm toward the ethnic ideology of *blanqueamiento*, whitening, the more comfortable Uruguayans will feel about the image they project to the world as a society without discernible African influence.

There is evident here a profound generational gap between Ester Arrascaeta and Florencia Gularte regarding the significance of the comparsa. The former relates it to "lo ancestral" while the latter views the ritual in terms of "lo comercial." Given the degree to which Carnaval and its many components, including the Llamadas, have become institutionalized and commercialized by the Montevideo power structure, Afro-Uruguayans stand to lose more vestiges of their ancestral cultural heritage.

As mentioned earlier, in the first volume of the *Antología de poetas negros uruguayos* (1990), Alberto Britos includes two poems by José Roberto Suárez devoted to the drum culture ("Tambor" amd "Parche y Madera") and another to "Barrio Reus al Sur." In these selections, Suárez touched upon themes dear to Afro-Uruguayans as the poetic voice interprets cultural maintenance and place and displacement. Britos situated the three aforementioned poems in the period between "1950 y 1960 que la temática del negro cobra fuerza"[16] ["1950 and 1960 that the black theme gains strength"].

As a matter of fact, the black theme had always been present in Suárez's creative vision: "Candombe," a poem published in 1946, is indicative of this tendency.[17] In this selection, Suárez questions the historic cultural significance of this ritual. The Candombe, for Suárez, carries a deeper meaning than present-day song and dance.

It incarnates aspects of the black experience from Africa to the Americas through an initial evocation of the horrors of slavery and a subsequent examination of the realities of displacement in Uruguay.

Reminiscencia . . .
De infeliz tiempo pasado
Que mi numen en esta hora evoca,
Oprobiosa y retrógada época de esclavos . . .
¡Maldición! . . . Imprecación que brota de mi boca.

El negro . . .
Trajo consigo
de la—selva umbría—
una danza . . .
Una danza . . .
Que en los días de bonanza
Era expresión de alegría
que bailaba con ternura
que sólo él comprendía...
Esa danza, de gravísima armonía.
¡Danza! . . .
Cuándo la vean bailar,
notarán que carece de alegría,
que es la galana ironía
que gasta al son del tambor . . .
Allí expresa su dolor
que está en plena rebeldía.
"Reyes" presiden la "fiesta"
se hace alarde de boato,
bailan torvos, con recato,
hacen rueda, palmotean . . .
Voces de origen corean
se arma una baraúnda,
entonan "endumba cunga"
"congo-luanda, ye, ye, ye,"
así es a grandes rasgos
el candombe, candombée . . .

Reminiscence . . .
Of an unhappy past
Which my inspiration at this time evokes,
Dishonest and reactionary era of slaves . . .
A curse! . . . Curse which springs from my mouth.

[The black . . .
Brought with him

from the—shady jungle—
a dance . . .
A dance . . .
Which on days of prosperity
Was an expression of happiness
which he danced with tenderness
which only he understood . . .
That dance, of very deep harmony.
Dance! . . .
When you see it performed,
you will note that it lacks happiness,
which is elegant irony
that is wasted to the sound of the drum . . .
Thus he expresses his pain
which is in open rebellion.
"Kings" preside over the "fiesta"
it is an impressive show
they dance grimly, with reserve
they make noise, they clap
Original voices sing
pandemonium breaks out
they sing "endumba cunga"
"congo-luanda, ye, ye, ye,"
thus with great gestures
the candombe, candombe . . .]

The "Candombe," according to the poetic voice, is a mask, a disguise to hide the true feelings of its performers. It has been transformed from a ritual of happiness and harmony in the transition from Africa to its present ironic form. The poetic voice makes it clear that there is a profound difference between the appearance and the reality of the ritual: "When you see it performed,/you will note that it lacks happiness,/which is elegant irony/that is wasted to the sound of the drum." The implication is that the subtle meaning of Candombe can be lost to those who do not understand the true meaning of the ritual which, in Uruguay, is one of resistance: "Thus he expresses his pain/which is in open rebellion".

Juan Julio Arrascaeta Jr., as mentioned earlier, is the contemporary Afro-Uruguayan poet who has interpeted on several occasions the phenomenon of Candombe. Some of his poems are in manuscript form and included in the second edition of the *Antología de poetas negros uruguayos* (1997): "Nací bailando candombe"/"I was Born Dancing Candombe," "Candombe bemba"/"Thick-Lipped

Candombe," "Que el candombe sea inmortal"/"May the Candombe be Immortal," and "Embrujo del candombe"/"The Spell of Candombe." These selections vary from surface interpretations to more profound meditations upon the meanings of this Afro-Uruguayan ritual. In this regard, "Nací bailando candombe" is the most representative of these poems:

Me preguntan si el candombe
a bailarlo lo aprendí
lo llevo impreso en el alma
desde el día en que nací

Corral, cajón de madera
palos de escoba el perfil
a mis sueños lo acunaron
los sones de un tamboril

Camino y sin darme cuenta
mi cuerpo voy balanceando
como si un compás lejano
el ritmo fuera marcando

El embrujo del candombe
todo en mi se posesiona
es la savia que da vida
a mi ser como persona.[18]

[They asked me if
I learned to dance the Candombe
I carry it imprinted on my soul
from the day I was born

An enclosure, a wooden box
broomsticks on the side
my dreams are rocked by
the sounds of a drum

I walk and without realizing
my body begins swaying
as if a far away beat
were marking the rhythm

The spell of the Candombe
possesses all of me
it is the sap which gives life
to my being as a person.]

Candombe, from the Afro-Uruguayan perspective of Arrascaeta, is not merely a dance. Rather, it is an art form that helps to define an ethnic identity. Dancing Candombe is just as "cultural" as learning how to play a drum. However, the attitudes of Repique, the informant discussed earlier, and Arrascaeta coincide to the extent that they believe there is something uniquely African derived in these activities.

The poetic voices discussed here historicize Candombe within the contexts of slavery and the struggle for liberation. The ritual connects the speakers to the mythic African homeland while underscoring the fact that Candombe brings to the surface ancestral longings. The issues of place and displacement remain major concerns. Arrascaeta's attitudes correspond to those expressed by Suárez to the extent that the writer as visionary is able to see beyond the surface and arrive at a clearer understanding of the Candombe, with its cultural codes and different levels of signification.

CARNAVAL

The incorporation of black ritual into mainstream Uruguayan society is an ongoing process that was noted by some experts in the 1950s. Paulo de Carvalho Neto approaches the topic from the perspectives of color and money in his analysis of the 1954 Carnaval in Montevideo. He states:

> Como consecuencia de la aparición de los premios hasta pueden comprobarse fenómenos de aculturaciones y, por ende, de mestizajes. Se observa durante los carnavalaes montevideanos de hoy, por ejemplo, cierto "anegramiento" blanco y cierto "blanqueamiento negro" . . . Los casos de "anegramiento" blanco son los tamborileros blancos y los lubolos, o sea, blancos pintados de negros. En cambio, entre los casos de "blanqueamiento" negro está la "bailarina." Bailarinas y coristas son cosas nuevas entre los negros, impuestas, en parte, por la intervención estatal. No integran el núcleo considerado "tradicional" de la comparsa lubola, el del candombe. Ellas son un atentado contra la belleza clásica de la "negra vieja," con sus trajes largos y adornados de estrellas. La "bailarina," imitando a la blanca, se presenta sólo con un traje mínimo de dos piezas. Inevitablemente, con sus prejuicios, el público piensa luego que es una "raza" intensamente sexual.[19]

> [As a consequence of the appearance of the prizes one can even verify them as phenomena of acculturation and, consequently, of misce-

genation. One observes during the Montividean carnavals today, for example, certain white "blackening" and certain black "whitening" . . . The examples of white blackening are the white drummers and the *lubolos*, that is, whites colored as blacks. On the other hand, among the examples of black "whitening" is the *bailarina*. Dancers and cho- rists are new things among blacks, imposed, in part, by state interven- tion. They are not integral to the "traditional" nucleus of the *comparsa lubola*, that of the Candombe. They are an effort against the classic beauty of the "old black woman" with her long dresses adorned with stars. The "bailarina," imitating the white woman, appears with only the minimum garment of two pieces. Inevitably, with its prejudices, the public then believes that it is a "race" intensely sexual.]

The degree to which the traditional structure of the Candombe has been altered to meet the financial exigencies of the Montevideo mu- nicipality has long been a concern of Afro-Uruguayans. The empha- sis upon the sexual and the exotic embodied in the vedette diminishes significantly the meaning of the comparsa.

It is generally accepted that Afro-Uruguayan participation in the activities of Carnaval was institutionalized in 1956 with the inclusion of the "Desfile de las Llamadas" by the Montevideo governing bodies. In reference to this ritual, Luis Ferreira explains:

> es el desfile de las asociaciones carnavalesca afrouruguayas tradi- cionales por los barrios Sur y Palermo, con antecedentes de desfile competetivo que datan de 1905. En 1956 el desfile fue oficializado por la Intendencia de Montevideo y denominado Desfile de Lla- madas; aclaramos que esta denominación no cantó con el consenso de la Asociación Cultural y Social Uruguay.[20]

> [it is the parade of traditional Afrouruguayan carnaval assocations through the neighborhoods of Sur and Palermo, with antecedents of competitive parades which date to 1905. In 1956 the parade was offi- cialized by the Municipality of Montevideo and labeled *Desfile de Lla- madas*; we must clarify that this denomination did not receive the consensus of ACSU.]

It is significant to note that ACSU opposed the removal of the most important visual manifestation of Afro-Uruguayan culture from black control. This final act of cooptation by City Hall in 1956 was the culmination of a long process of official intrusion. In fact, the at- tempt to officialize Afro-Uruguayan particpation during Carnaval began as early as 1911. In an editorial entitled "La Comisión de Fiestas y la Sociedad de Color"/ "The Commission of Events and Colored Society," which appeared in *La Verdad*, the writer states:

> Merece un aplauso sincero y entusiasta la Comisión de Fiestas por la simpática actitud asumida al incluir en su programa a la colectividad de color, asignándole un puesto en los festejos y facilitándonos los medios para su realización.[21]

> [The Commission of Events deserves a sincere and enthusiastic round of applause for the kind attitude assumed by including in its program the colored community, assigning us a place in the festivities and facilitating for us the means to achieve our goals.]

Afro-Uruguayan ability to take advantage of this offer was obstructed by the bickering and infighting, as reported in the press, among the different clubs and special interests. *La Verdad* continued its annual coverage of Carnaval from 1911–14, documenting community involvement as well as acts by individuals.

The contemporary black press, however, has often been critical of the phenomenon of Carnaval. *Nuestra Raza*, in particular, was harsh in its appraisal of the motives of the planners and the participants. A few examples will serve to illustrate. Iris M. Cabral, a columnist and social activist, wrote:

> Al ritmo loco del candombe que es una expresión misma del negro, yo he visto un desfile de máscaras ridículas ... Esto es lo que veo, bufonadas que divierten al bufón. Carnaval que ridiculiza al verdadero carnaval, al antiguo de nuestros abuelos, menos aparatoso pero lleno de más sana alegría.[22]

> [To the crazy rhythm of the Candombe, which is a true expression of black people, I have seen a parade of ridiculous masks. This is what I see, clowning which entertains the clown. A carnival which ridicules the true carnival, the old one of our forefathers, less showy but filled with more heartfelt happiness.]

This new Carnaval is lacking in spirituality, it seems and does not reflect Afro-Uruguayan values. In an ironic commentary entitled, "Exaltación Lubola"/"African Exaltation" in a subsequent number of *Nuestra Raza*, Mario L. Montero, an editorial writer, observes:

> Y pasa el lubolo, arrastrando el pasado, pletórico de cintas, estrellas, y rituales, reverdeciendo en sus sones plañideros o salvajes, nostálgi-

cas leyendas que nos habla de añares y añares de esclavitud, sufrida desde el expatrio cruel del Africa costera y querida.[23]

[And the African passes, dragging the past, overflowing with ribbons, stars, and rituals, basking in their mournful or savage songs, nostalgic legends that speak to us of years and years of slavery, suffered since the cruel expatriation from dear and coastal Africa.]

Behind the masks, Montero is able to see some of the pain of the Afro-Uruguayan experience, which cannot be disguised, superficially, by an outward manifestation of happiness that occurs once a year. The profundity of the message that the "Lubolo" is attemtping to convey to the public is trivialized by the less serious elements of Carnaval.

The African dimension of Uruguayan Carnaval is contextualized in a more meaningful way the following year (1940):

¡Antes Carnaval! Por los caminos del Atlántico, en las bodegas sin aire de los barcos negreros llegó a América el Carnaval, nuestro Carnaval. Viejo como el tiempo, tiene de una antigua civilización el alma africana. La farsa vive en la lonja del tamboril templada a fuego; vibra al impulso endiablado de la mano del negro que la toca y le infunde un poco de su propio humano dolor, cambiado en música, en canto, en algarabia bulliciosa, medio selva y medio fuego . . . Pasó. Hoy el carnaval es dolor que no se puede imponer a la alegría, porque degeneró en comercio.[24]

[Before Carnival! Along the routes of the Atlantic, in the airless holds of the slave ships, Carnival, our Carnival arrived in America. As old as time, the African soul has an ancient civilization. The farce lives in the leather of the drum tuned with fire; the satanic impulse of the hand of the black man who plays it and infuses a bit of his own human pain, changed in music, in song, in boisterous gibberish, half jungle and half fire . . . It happened. Today Carnival is pain which cannot be imposed upon happiness, because it has degenerated into commerce.]

Writing in the 1930s and '40s, Afro-Uruguayan intellectuals demonstrated uncanny foresight into the commercial direction of Carnaval and the degree to which it would appropriate Afro-Uruguayan culture. Carnaval as an ancestral ritual has been supplanted by exploitation for material gains is the point made by Cabral and Montero and further emphasized by other editorial writers in the black press.

Most recently, in an opinion piece published in *Mundo Afro*, Guillermo Rosas, a columnist, has called for a more equitable distribution of the profits from Carnaval, since the momentum toward commercialization will only intensify. He questions:

> ¿A dónde van a parar esas ganancias? ¿Qué le aportan a nuestra cultura? ¿Qué ley nos protege para que lo nuestro no sea violado así porque sí? Un montón de gente hace dinero gracias a la fiesta, menos aquellos que realmente lo merecen: los hacedores de ella. Llegó el momento de ponerle punto final. ¡Basta! ¡Exijamos lo que nos pertenece! Debe ser aprobada una legislación que regule el entorno y que resguarde sobre la comercialización de esa fiesta que nos pertenece.[25]

> [Where are these earnings going to end up? What do they contribute to our culture? What law protects us so that what is ours will not be violated just for the sake of it? A large number of people make money thanks to the party, except for those who deserve it: the makers of it. The time has come to end it. Enough! We demand what belongs to us. Legislation has to be approved which regulates the activity and safeguards the commercialization of that activity which belongs to us.]

Rosas is merely reiterating what black Uruguayans have been saying for decades. The possibility of collective action by the Comparsas to benefit themselves is hindered by the competitive aspect of the business as well as the conflictive nature of the Afro-Uruguayans, who cannot agree on an effective way to remedy this situation.

Given the current symbiotic relationship between Carnaval and the comparsas, Luis Ferreira's analysis is on the mark: "Podemos concluir que la política cultural estatal en esta área se ha caracterizado, básicamente, por un solo interés en la venta de un espectáculo para su consumo" ["We can conclude that political state culture in this area is characterized, basically, by a single interest in the sale of a spectacle for its consumption"] (44).

Afro-Uruguayans are caught "between a rock and a hard place" within the Carnaval culture. Should monetary gain be subordinated to ancestral memory? The level of cultural syncretism apparent in the Carnaval of today indicates that Afro-Uruguayans are clinging tenaciously to aspects of their heritage and using it, as much as possible, to their benefit.

LITERARY INTERPRETATIONS

It is only fitting at this point to recognize the importance of Rosa Luna, the internationally renowned Vedette, in the evolution of Carnaval, Candombe, and the drum culture. Rosa Luna, who died almost a decade ago, lived the black Uruguayan experience to its fullest, a life that is captured in the book, *Rosa Luna: sin tanga y sin tongo.* In "El conventillo," the initial chapter, the author tells us:

Tuve la suerte de nacer en el Medio Mundo, en Cuareim entre Durazno e Isla de Flores. Allí donde los morenos de mi raza repiqueteaban los tambores noche a noche y hacían temblar las paredes de construcción antigua.[26]

[I was lucky to be born in Medio Mundo, on Cuareim between Durazno and Isla de Flores. There where the blacks of my race played the drums night after night and made the walls of the old construction shake.]

Subsequent chapters take the reader on a voyage through Rosa Luna's childhood, adolescence, adulthood, and emergence as an international Uruguayan cultural icon. Throughout this first-person narration, the author does not deviate from her posture as an advocate of Afro-Uruguayan cultural traditions. Rosa Luna places herself at the center of the Carnaval tradition alongside such legendary figures as "la Negra" Johnson and Martha Gularte.

Throughout *Rosa Luna: sin tanga y sin tongo,* in addition to an astute awareness of the social position of Afro-Uruguayans, a perceptive awareness of national and international affairs is evident. There has been a great deal of soul-searching amongst Afro-Uruguayans in relation to the displacement of black people from the Barrio Sur. Rosa Luna presented an answer: "También fuimos cobardes cuando nos despojaran del Medio Mundo o Ansina. ¿Qué hicimos por mantenerlos en pie?" ["We were also cowards when they threw us out of Medio Mundo or Ansina. What did we do to stand on our feet?"] (66). Historically, there was a minimum of Afro-Uru-guayan resistance to these acts. Instead they continued to see them-selves as victims of a political process over which they had no control.

Rosa Luna maintains a strong sense of self and ethnic identity throughout her autobiography as evinced in this self portrait:

Me llamo Rosa Amelia Luna,
nací allá por los años
cuarenta, bajo el signo de
Géminis, en el Barrio Palermo
Barrio de negros . . . y blancos,
de Candombes . . . y tangos,
de tristezas muchas y alegrías pocas,
boliches de vino, y calles angostas . . .
El resto, es una historia larga . . .

(11)

[My name is Rosa Amelia Luna,
I was born sometime in the
forties, under the sign of
Gemini, in Barrio Palermo
A barrio of blacks . . . and whites
of Candombes . . . and tangos,
of much sadness and few joys
clubs with wine, and narrow streets . . .
The rest is a long story . . .

The "long story" depicted in *Rosa Luna: sin tanga y sin tongo* is representative of the black experience in Uruguay, not just in terms of Carnaval and Candombe, but also to the degree that the seminal role of the Barrio Sur in the formation of Afro-Uruguayan cultural traditions is foregrounded. Her sense of the creation of cultural space is shared by other authors as well.

In his attempt to contextualize the Llamadas of February 1999, which synthesizes the best of Carnaval and Candombe, "Redoblante" (Nelson Domínguez)—the columnist for *El País* writes:

El palpitar de la negritud recreando, a manera de un tan gigantesco como admirable espectáculo callejero, una historia cuyos orígenes afloran entre las brumas de los tiempos.

¡Tu . . . tucutúm bambá! . . . ¡borocotó chás! . . . chás! repicando hasta el cielo como para rendir tributo a la vuelta de las generaciones, a la primera vez que la palabra candombe aparecía mencionada públicamente en un periódico local.

Como históricamente occuría en 1834 para celebrar con alborozo el fin de la esclavitud oprobiosa de los negros africanos traídos a estas costas por los infames mercaderes y mercenarios de la carne humana. ¡Candombe!, sí . . . símbolo auténtico de un perfil intimamente nuestro que se menionaba inicialmente por entonces como parte del "Canto Patriótico de los Negros," cuya autoría se la atribuyó a Francisco Acuña de Figueroa, creador del Himno Nacional.[27]

[The pulse of blackness re-creating, such a gigantic as well as admirable street spectacle, a history whose origins crop up among the mists of all time. ¡Tu . . . tucutúm bambá! . . . ¡borocotó chás! . . . chás! resounding to heaven as if to pay homage to the cycle of generations, to the first time the word "candombe" appeared mentioned publicly in a local periodical.

As it historically occurred in 1834 to celebrate with merriment the end of the opprobrious enslavement of black Africans brought to these shores by the vile mercenaries and traders of human flesh. Candombe! yes . . . authentic symbol of a profile intimately ours which was mentioned initially back then as part of the "Patriotic Song of the Blacks" whose authorship has been attributed to Francisco Acuña de Figueroa, creator of the National Hymn.]

The Tambor, Candombe, Carnaval, and the Llamadas, it seems, from this perspective, are as integral components of the Uruguayan cultural fabric as the National Anthem. As we enter the new millennium, is it too much to request that the Afro-Uruguayans, whose experiences generated these aspects of national culture, be afforded the rewards, privileges, and respect that have eluded them for more than a century?

4

Resistance and Identity
in Afro-Uruguayan Poetry

IT IS USEFUL TO BEGIN THIS DISCUSSION OF AFRO-URUGUAYAN POETRY
with some pertinent ideas regarding identity, subject construction,
and postcoloniality from Jonathan Culler and Homi Bhabha. Culler
writes: "A lot of recent theoretical debate concerns the identity and
function of the subject or self. What is this 'I' that I am—person,
agent or actor, self—and what makes it what it is? Two basic questions
underlie modern thinking on this topic: first, is the self something
given or something made and, second, should it be conceived in individual or in social terms?"[1] In the historical process of the construction of an Afro-Uruguayan identity, the "subject" has always
been the result of a combination of an agent who both makes
choices and has them imposed by cultural factors (social, economic,
psychological). The Afro-Uruguayan self, as represented literarily, is
a conflictive relationship between "something given" and "something made" that is conceived in both individual and social terms.
Writers do not see a clear-cut dichotomy in the relationship between
individual and society. Therefore, the historical Afro-Uruguayan situation is difficult to assess, theoretically and practically, due to individual and collective dynamics, as well as the nature of their society.

In *The Location of Culture*, Homi K. Bhabha employs "two post-
colonial portraits" (Adil Jussawalla and Edward Said) to elaborate
upon,

> two familiar traditions in the discourse of identity: the philosophical
> tradition of identity as the process of self-reflection in the mirror of
> (human) nature; and the anthropological view of the difference of
> human identity as located in the division of Nature/Culture. In the

postcolonial text the problem of identity returns as a persistent questioning of the frame, the space of representation, where the image—
missing person, invisible eye, Oriental stereotype—is confronted
with its difference, its Other.[2]

Afro-Uruguayan writers operate within the two traditions—philo-
sophical and anthropological— outlined by Bhabha. There is the
process of self-reflection as well as ethnic differentiation. In the "persistent questioning of the frame," self-identification in an internally
colonized situation leads to a double level of "otherness"—who am I?
and how am I perceived by the majority culture? Afro-Uruguayan
writers from Timoteo Olivera to Cristina Rodríguez Cabral have addressed the issue of identity in serious fashion, through an assertion
of their humanity and a resistance to marginality.

In spite of the general attitude toward the black experience in
Uruguay, which often espouses the idea that existence was not as difficult in that country as in some others, many Afro-Uruguayan writers
disagree with the official story. Writing against the grain, in opposition to mainstream perceptions, has been the approach by creative
writers from the early appearance of Black periodicals such as *La
Conservación* to published writers of the present day. In newspapers,
journals, and books, there is an Afro-Uruguayan literary tradition—
poetry, for the most part—that affirms many positive values of the
black community. This creative writing supports the sentiments of es-
sayists and social activists in their search for freedom and dignity
through an affirmation of a black identity. Subsequently resistance
and the construction of self are fundamental issues in Afro-
Uruguayan poetry.

In its narrowest definition, "Afro-Uruguayan poetry" is written by
blacks, about blacks, for blacks and society in general, and not "negrista" poems written by other ethnic groups with good or bad intentions. The difference is that with Afro-Uruguayan poets there is a
strong identification by the poetic "I" with the experience treated.
The black subject, instead of being a mere object of the poetic discourse, is an integral part of the expression of sentiments from
within. My views on Afro-Uruguayan poetry differ from those of Alberto Britos, who in his three anthologies of "black" poetry, includes
both black and nonblack writers.[3]

In her classic study of literature of the African diaspora, Martha
Cobb has shown how the four basic concepts of confrontation, dual-
ism, identity, and liberation connect writers temporally and spatially.[4]

Underlying these concepts is the issue of resistance, an attempt at self-definition and an effort, by Afro-Uruguayans, to avoid marginalization. The articulations of opposition to the status quo begins with the poems of Timoteo Olivera, which appeared in *La Conservación* in 1872. In "A los hombres de color"/"To Men of Color," Olivera initiates a poetic discourse which has lasted to our day. This poem was dedicated to the founding of Club Igualdad, whose objective was the improvement of the Afro-Uruguayan condition because:

> En la uruguaya región
> Un pueblo morada había
> Pueblo que infeliz jemía
> Bajo una dura opresión
>
> Componíase este pueblo
> De los hombres de color
> Que ni aun derecho tenían
> Para levantar la voz.[5]
>
> [In the Uruguayan region
> A people lived there
> A people who unhappily grieved
> Under harsh oppression
>
> This people was composed
> Of men of color
> Who did not even have the right
> To raise their voice.]

The poetic voice expresses an existential anguish caused by physical oppression, as well as mental distress. This psychological dilemma is occasioned by basic social contradictions:

> Estamos en un país libre;
> Y no encuentro yo razón
> El que estemos oprimidos
> Tan solo por el color.
>
> [We are in a free country;
> And I do not find a reason
> Why we are oppressed
> Only because of color.]

Subsequently, there is a virile call for resistance:

O si la hora ha llegado
Luchemos pues con valor,
Que si hemos de ser ovejas,
Ser lobos será mejor.

Halcemos alcemos alta la frente
Y aun más alta nuestra voz.
Que ya no somos esclavos
Que somos hombres de honor.

[Or if the hour has arrived
Let's fight with valor,
Since if we must be sheep
To be wolves will be better.

Lift up lift up our countenance
And even louder our voice
Because now we are not slaves
Rather we are men of color.]

This rhetoric of resistance, so prevalent in the pages of *La Conservación*, advances the idea that force is necessary to assure the rights of Afro-Uruguayans that were won during the wars of independence. "A la raza de color"/"To the Colored Race," a poem from *La Conservación* discussed earlier, also places the blame for discrimination against blacks squarely with the white oppressor.

Carlos Cardozo Ferreira, José Roberto Suárez, Pilar Barrios, Virginia Brindis de Salas, Juan Julio Arrascaeta Sr. and Cristina Rodríguez Cabral are but a few of the twentieth-century poets who build upon the pioneering work of their predecessors affiliated with *La Conservación*, where the basis for contemporary Afro-Uruguayan poetry is established. Cardozo Ferreira, in "Negro en la noche"/"Black Man in the Night," and "Invitación a negrita"/"Invitation to a Black Woman," two poems published in *Nuestra Raza* in 1936, treats the theme of the affirmation of black identity. The former poem is an introspective piece which presents the Black as an entity that always carries a part of Africa internally. In "Black Man in the Night," the "tamboril" is the symbol of connectiveness, as the color black becomes a metaphor of survival:

Es el corazón del negro
un tamboril en la noche
vieja como su prejuicio,
un tamboril,

en su corazón,
en llamada frenética
a su luna de amor.
   Rosa negra de la noche
para el ojal de su boca
media luna de risa
   Entelequía del negro
nutrida de hostilidad sistemática.
   Entelequía del negro
consustanciada en la color
cósmica en la Noche . . .
piel para su espiritualidad.[6]

[The heart of the black man
is a drum in the night
old as its prejudice,
a drum,
in his heart,
in a frenetic call
to its moon of love.
   Black rose of the night
for the eyelet of your mouth
half moon of your smile
   Élan vital of the black man
nurtured in systematic hostility
   Élan vital of the black man
consubstantiated in the cosmic
color of Night . . .
skin for his spirituality.]

The metaphor of the heart as a drum highlights a cultural identity
marker that reinforces the cosmic blend that the poetic voice sees between blackness and the universe. As a vital force controlling growth
and life, the heart is just as vital as color to black survival. Night does
not hinder the black man but rather serves as a background for for-
mulating acts of resistance.

   "Invitation to a Black Woman" presents a dancer proud of her
color and with her black identity emphasized. The apostrophic encounter occurs within the context of Carnaval:

   Ponte presto,
tu traje de colores, mi negrita/
Mi negrita,
tú sabes

que Momo es un viejo vesánico sensual
que tiene su corazón en ritmo de candombe
y que pide
y te dan
y nunca está contento.
    ¡Ponte presto,
tu traje de colores, mi negrita!
Tu debes reir, reirte mucho.
Me enerva el triunfo de tu cuerpo
estatua de carne
flor de vida!
Es inefable
la escala musical de tu risa.
Suena el tam tam, mi negrita/
Ponte presto tu traje de colores,
jungla de tu pelo,
corazón de tus labios,
noche tropical de tus ojos
misteriosos y quemantes . . .
Cocos de tus senos! . . .
Quisiera un selvático escenario
y danzando gozar
en el triunfo de tu danza . . .[7]

[Get ready,
your bright dress, my little black one/
My darling
you know
that Momo is an old sensual crazy
who has his heart in tune to candombe
and who asks for
and they give to you
and he is never content.
    Get ready,
your bright dress, my darling!
You must smile, smile a lot
The lavishness of your body weakens me
statue of flesh
flower of life!
The musical height of your smile
is untouchable.
The tam tam sounds, my darling/
Put on your bright dress,
jungle of your hair
heart of your lips

tropical night of your eyes
mysterious and burning . . .
Coconut-like breasts! . . .
I would like a wild and dancing
scenario to enjoy
the triumph of your dance . . .]

This poem is anticipatory in nature as the poetic voice attempts to inspire the black female subject to perform to maximum capacity during Carnaval, under the watchful gaze of "Momo," the symbolic representation of unrestricted passion and joy. The physical presence presented in this scene is a positive one as the "negrita" is connected to her African origins, while at the same time displaying attributes that are positive from head to toe. The negrita is placed in a rhetorical African context, to the extent that the references are at the surface level. The mode of address, apostrophe, is ambivalent because on the one hand, she is objectified, while at the same time reminded of positive qualities associated with her roots.

Some of the poetry of Juan Julio Arrascaeta Sr. and Pilar E. Barrios belong to this same tradition of affirmation of blackness and resistance. For instance, in two poems by Arrascaeta, blacks and whites are juxtaposed unflatteringly. "La negrita"/"Black Girl" treats the issue of revenge by a servant taken upon a cruel owner. She has arranged for some errant garment pins to prick the master's wife at a party, a covert way of getting even. The poetic voice explains:

No fue el pícaro ratón
ni travesura, ni chanza
sino es mi venganza
por la paliza que ayer me dio.[8]

[It was not the wily mouse
nor a prank, nor luck
but it is my vengeance
for the beating he gave me yesterday.]

Since overt action against those in power is not possible, the servant must use the means at hand to assume a degree of agency. Resistance to domination takes multiple forms in this Afro-Uruguayan context. "Black Girl," which begins with the refrain, "¡Ja . . . Ja . . . Ja! hay que risa me da"/ ["how it makes me laugh"] is deceptive, because the light tone masks the deeper message that through subversive action protests the treatment of blacks.

"La Muñeca"/"The Doll" addresses the issue of black identity:

Es muy linda la muñeca
que amita a la niña le regaló
tiene sandunga y es negrita como soy yo.

Tiene dientes blancos de marfil,
su boquita punzó dice mamá,
sus ojos lloran sin lágrimas como lloro yo.

Tiene regios vestidos llenos de cintas,
una camita de sábanas
blancas, más blancas que las que tengo yo.

¡Ah . . . Señor, tú que estás en el cielo
traéme una muñeca negrita
de boquita punzó, que diga mamá,
con ojos sin lágrimas y mucha sandunga
y no sea esclava como soy yo![9]

[The doll is very pretty
which missy gave the child
she has style and is black like me

It has teeth white as ivory
its little puckered mouth says mama
its eyes cry without tears like me.

It has regal clothes full of ribbons
a little bed with white
sheets, whiter than those I have.

Ah! . . . Father who is in heaven
bring me a little black doll
with a puckered mouth, who says mama,
with eyes without tears and much presence
and not a slave like me.]

The poetic voice is that of an innocent slave child who identifies with the doll but does not wish her gift to share the burden of slavery. In the form of a prayer, in an ironic tone, the narrator protests her personal situation in a deceptively naive way. The poetic voice recognizes the impotence of the two parallel situations that she believes only a higher power can remedy.

"Raza negra"/"Black Race" by Pilar Barrios is one of his first poems treating the African experience in the Americas. It is a selection designed to embrace the diaspora experience in an encompassing fashion:

Abrete cual río murmurante,
iniciate tu misma en el camino.
Sed, de tu propia nave su marino
para llevarla enhiesta hacia adelante.

Hazte apta, dinámica y pujante,
digna y capaz de influir en tu destino.
Cincel modelador, vibrante himno
de una fuerza viril y avasallante.

Por el martirologio que tuviste
por toda la ignominia que sufriste
en el dolor de tus antepasados;

yo, te exhorto a luchar firme y de frente
llevando hacia el futuro del presente,
todos los adelantos alcanzados![10]

[Open up like a babbling brook,
set out on the road.
Be the sailor of your own ship
in order to carry it upright toward the future.

Be clever, dynamic and strong,
proud and capable of influencing your destiny.
Modeler's chisel, resonant hymn
of a virile and overpowering force.

For the martyrdom that you suffered
for the shame you suffered in the
pain of your ancestors;

I implore you to fight hard and face to face
carrying toward the future of the present
all the progress realized!]

The poetic voice in this sonnet makes a connection between past and present in an effort to focus better upon the needs of the future. The pain and suffering of the black ancestors is not to be repeated. As a point of comparison, the poetic rhetoric of Barrios is not as direct as that of Timoteo Olivera for instance, but both carry the same message, that is, "fight hard and face to face." The message is take control of your own destiny, leave the unglorious past behind, and forge a meaningful future. The horror of slavery, which will not be forgotten, can serve as a powerful motivational tool for subsequent generations.

While Virginia Brindis de Salas (1908–1958) is one of the most well-known of the Afro-Uruguayan writers, she is also one of the most controversial. In the introduction to the *Antología de poetas negras uruguayos* (1990), the late Alberto Britos Serrat, the editor, maintains:

> Los dos libros de Virginia Brindis de Salas merecen nuestra duda, confirmada por las declaraciones de los promotores de los mismos y del verdadero autor de ellos. Este fenómeno es más frecuente de lo que se puedan imaginar los lectores, en el Uruguay y en otros países, motivo por el cual no queremos entrar en detalles ya perimidos, y que indujeron a error a mucha gente de buena fe.[11]

> [The two books by Virginia Brindis de Salas warrant our doubt, confirmed by the promoters of them and their true author. This phenomenon is more frequent than the readers can imagine, in Uruguay and in other countries, a motive for which we do not wish to enter into obsolete details, and which cause many people of good faith to error.]

I am one of the people of good faith since I devoted a chapter to the poetry of Pilar Barrios and Virginia Brindis de Salas in my study, *Afro-Hispanic Poetry 1940–1980: From Slavery to "Negritud" in South American Verse* (1983). Before writing that book, I researched Afro-Uruguayan periodicals of that historical period and there was no indication that Virginia Brindis de Salas was not the author of the two books that carry her name. If Julio Guadalupe, with whom I communicated before writing the book regarding copyright permissions and as an intellectual involved with black journals, is in reality the author, and not the editor, of *Pregón de Marimorena/The Song of Mary Morena* (1946) and *Cien cárceles de amor/One Hundred Love Ballads* (1949), he has much to explain to the academic community regarding the ethics of publishing. In a subsequent meeting with Alberto Britos in his study regarding Virginia Brindis de Salas and authorship, no concrete evidence was presented to deny her authorship.

In the three volumes of the *Antología de poetas negros uruguayos*, Alberto Britos, the editor, engaged in a campaign to write Virginia Brindis de Salas out of Uruguayan literary history. In the first volume, Julio Guadalupe, Britos's old friend, is listed as the author of "Canto para un muchacho negro americano del sur"/"Song for a Black American Boy from the South," which Brindis de Salas published in *Pregón de Marimorena*. In the introduction to the second volume,

Britos justifies the exclusion of both Brindis de Salas and Guadalupe in the following manner:

> De Montevideo, de un amigo de la infancia que no desea le publique más sus poemas por razones sociopolíticas y de los segundos por no poder interpretar nuestra realidad a raíz de la exclusión en el primer tomo del nombre de una señora que aparece como escritora y no lo era y en favor de mi posición voy acumulando pruebas lentamente, pues para nosotros los que vivimos la trayectoria de esa persona nos resulta clarísimo nuestra prescindencia.[12]

> [From Montevideo, from a childhood friend who does not wish me to publish more of his poems because of sociopolitical reasons and secondly for not being able to interpret our reality based upon the exclusion in the first volume of the name of a woman who seems to be a writer but was not and in support of my position I continue accumulating proofs slowly, thus for those of us who lived the trajectory of that person our perspective remains very clear.]

Also in this volume, Britos attributes to José Carlos Santos Barbosa "Navidad Palermitana," which was published in *Cien cárceles de amor* by Brindis de Salas. At the same time, Britos accuses Brindis de Salas of plagiarizing the Dominican poet, Manuel del Cabral, whom Britos erroneously refers to as "portorriqueño."

Britos bases his evidence against Brindis de Salas on an interview with Beatriz Santos by Santos Barbosa and published in *Historias de Vida: Negros en el Uruguay* (1994). Barbosa explains:

> Y como tenía que entregarle una oda en su honor a doña Virginia de Salas, se la doy y ella la publicó en su segundo libro, *Cien cárceles de amor*. Le digo, "mire lo que hice ayer," y se lo mostré y me dice: "Qué lindo Carlitos, se lo voy a llevar a Pintín (Castellanos) que es loco por estas cosa." Cuando publica el libro había incluido mi "Navidad palermitana."[13]

> [And since I had to submit an ode in her honor to Ms. Virginia de Salas, I gave it to her and she published it in her second book, *Cien cárceles de amor*. I say to her, "look at what I did yesterday," and showed it to her and she says: "How beautiful Carlitos, I am going to give it to Pintín (Castellanos) who is crazy about these things." When the book was published she had included my "Navidad palermitana."]

Santos Barbosa goes on to state that he read some of del Cabral's works: "Y ahí veo que del Caudal [*sic*] ha escrito unos poemas que esa Doña Virginia publica como suyos ahí, y eso fue una cosa que me dejó fastidiado" ["And there I see that del Caudal has written some poems that Miss Virigina published as her own, and that was one thing which left me angry"]. In the first place, we have no way of comparing what Santos Barbosa wrote with what Brindis de Salas published. In the second place, a careful textual examination of the poetry of Manuel del Cabral, the Dominican poet, and Virginia Brindis de Salas reveals that she did *not* plagiarize any of his poems.

The change in attitude of Alberto Britos toward Virginia Brindis de Salas is difficult to explain, since when *Pregón de Marimorena*, her first book, appeared in 1946, he wrote:

> Virginia Brindis de Salas es nuestra primera y única poetisa negra quizá de todas estas regiones y se presenta con un libro lleno de hermosura, rebeldías y conciencia revelada, alerta, captando su posición de lucha como la de todas las conciencias conscientes, válgame la redundancia . . . De un ritmo acelerado, plenos de musicalidad todos sus poemas tienen un encanto nuevo. De rebeldía, de justicia, de cantos, de sones y formas de ciudad y selva, de campo y de fábrica de calle y de café.[14]

> [Virginia Brindis de Salas is our first and only black woman poet and perhaps of all of these regions and presents a book filled with beauty, rebellions, and an alert revealed conscience, earning her combative positions like that of all conscious consciences, excuse the redundance . . . With an accelerated rhythm, filled with musicality all of her poems have a new enchantment. About rebellion, about justice, about songs, about sounds and forms of city and jungle, about outdoors and about industry from street to street.]

This is the most positive review of Brindis de Salas's poetry written at the time it was published. If Virginia Brindis de Salas were a fraud, she certainly went undetected by her peers. She was celebrated throughout the Afro-Uruguayan community as a poet, leading intellectual, and stellar figure of the Círculo de Intelectuales, Artistas, Periodistas, y Escritores Negros (CIAPEN).

In fact, it was in Melo where Virginia Brindis de Salas was first recognized as a poet. Known as Iris Virginia Salas, her poem "Mi Corazón" (del libro próximo a aparecer)/"My Heart" (from the book soon to be published) first appeared in *Acción*, a leading Afro-Uruguayan journal:

Dije a mi corazón: estás cansado
como águila en prisión odias la vida
Si es cierto en tí la ilusión perdida,
Se esfumó con la sombra del pasado

¡Yo te sé luchador pujante y bravo!
¡Y eres tan fuerte y viril como el acero!;
¿No ha palpitado en ti sangre de esclavos?
¿Por qué vibras la lira estremecida?
¿Por qué no te libertas de tus rejas?
              ¡Y habló mi corazón;
              amo y espero . . . !
                         Iris Virginia Salas[15]

[I said to my heart: you're tired
like an eagle in prison you hate life
If it is true in you the lost illusion
evaporated with the shadow of the past

I know you are a fierce and brave fighter!
And you are as strong and virile as steel!;
Has the blood of slaves not pumped in you?
Why does your lyre sound so strident?
Why don't you free yourself from your cages?
              And my heart spoke!
              I love and I wait . . . !

"My heart" addresses one of the recurring themes in Afro-Uruguayan poetry, resistance to oppression and the constant desire for liberation. The speaker calls for overt, rather than more sublimated action.

Acción also published "Tus ojos"/"Your Eyes" by "Iris" and, in an editorial, took credit from some of her success on the publication of *Pregón de Marimorena*:

Iris, a quien fuimos los primeros en llamarle poetisa cuando ella visitó por primera vez nuestra ciudad nos hizo entregar de un manojo de poemas de su producción de los que hemos publicado algunos; es también uno de nuestros valores actuales, descendiente de una familia de gran renombre en los círculos del intelecto.[16]

[Iris, who we were the first to call poetess when she visited our city for the first time, gave us a handful of poems from her production of which we have published some; she is also one of our present treasures, a descendant of a family of great renown in intellectual circles.]

That "Iris" appropriated the Brindis de Salas name is certainly not the first time this has been done—nor the last, for that matter. What is important is that recent attempts to discredit Virginia Brindis de Salas have not been successful because in her time, she was recognized as an outstanding poet and a solid citizen.

In her writing, Virginia Brindis de Salas projected a strong sense of self as a black woman and an awareness of the importance of her African background. "Cantos"/"Songs" and "Negro: siempre triste"/ "Black Man: Always Sad" from *Cien cárceles de amor* will serve to illustrate the concerns. The former poem treats African origins and the latter, black identity. In "Songs" the poetic voice proclaims:

> En los bosques seculares
> del Africa Virginal
> Donde el león y el fiero chacal
> aterran al colibrí.
> Con las aves de los trópicos
> hace el plumaje altanero.
> Y donde canta el jilguero,
> allí fué donde nací.
> Si el sol, sol tostó
> a mi frente, no igual a
> mi corazón.
> A la inspiración
> de esta gran familia humana.
> Aprendiendo los deberes
> negros: no rechacen los placeres
> que ensanchan al corazón.[17]

> [In the secular forests
> of Virginal Africa
> Where the lion and the fierce jackal
> terrify the hummingbird.
> Where the tropical birds
> makes its haughty plumage.
> And where the goldfinch sings,
> that's where I was born.
> If the sun, the sun tanned
> my face, it is not the same
> for my heart.
> To the inspiration
> of the great human family.
> Learning black
> responsibilities: don't reject the pleasures
> which broaden the heart.]

"Songs" is "rhetorical" in its interpretation of Africa. The image projected is one of an imagined paradise filled with peace and harmony as well as violence in the nonhuman realm. Although "black" on the surface, the poetic voice speaks of a kind heart and deeds that inspire humanity, while: "that's where I was born" places it squarely at the center of the black experience.

"Black Man: Always Sad" is a cry for freedom and a call for inspiration to change the status quo:

> Tristezas de negros
> > tu canto es dolor, silencio,
> > > humildad.
> No cruces los brazos;
> > los negros no deben cruzarlos
> > > jamás.
> Tus antepasados los cruzaron ya . . .
> > Por temor al amor, por esclavitud
> > > negro triste olvida . . .
> Los buques negreros, aquellas sentinas oscuras
> > del barco, horrores, el hambre,
> > > azotes sufridos, olvídalo todo;
> > > > ¡que lentamente viene, la ansiada libertad!
>
> > Yo negra soy
> > Porque tengo la piel negra
> > ¡Esclava no!...
> > Yo nací de vientre libre.
> > Badagris Badagris, dictador
> > de la puñalada y el veneno.
> > Espíritu vuelto de los cañaverales
> > del Tafiá, Padre del rencor
> > y de la ira,
> > negro: implora al
> > Legbá, Dembolá, Uedó, Avidá.
> > Yo negra soy,
> > Porque tengo la piel negra
> > ¡Esclava no!...

(32)

> [Sadness of blacks
> > your song is pain, silence,
> > > humility.
> Don't cross your arms;
> > blacks must never
> > > cross them.

Your ancestors already gave up . . .
  For fear of love, for slavery
    sad black man forget . . .
The slave ships, those dark holes
  of the ship, horrors, hunger,
    beatings suffered, forget all of it;
    slowly comes the awaited freedom!

I am a black woman
Because I have black skin
A slave, no! . . .
I was born of a free womb.
Badagris, Badagris, dictator
of sword and venom.
Returned spirit of the cane fields
of Tafiá, Father of hate
and of rage,
black man: implore
Legbá, Dembolá, Uedó, Avidá.
I am a black woman
Because I have black skin
A slave, no! . . .

This poem is a challenge to blacks to radically change their perception of themselves and the world in which they live. Essentially the
work is divided into two parts: the first deploring slavery and its lasting impact upon black people, and the second affirming a strong
black female identity. Sadness, pain, silence, humility are the states of
being associated with black people in the initial verses. The second
tercet is, however, in defiant opposition to the first, as blacks are im-
plored not to accept passively their plight—"Don't cross your
arms"—and not to let the historical reality of slavery determine the
lives of free people. "Forget it all," the atrocities of slavery because
"slowly comes the long-awaited freedom!"

Being black does not necessarily make one a slave, the poetic
voice affirms. Blackness is a mental state, an identity that has to be
accepted and dealt with in order to advance socially. Otherwise, unless present-day blacks help themselves—"don't cross your arms"—
they will not advance because "Your ancestors already gave up." In
other words, one has to resist marginalization and fight for equality,
which has to be earned—not given. The message in this poem is that
in spite of the taking of African prisoners, the Middle Passage, slavery, and discrimination, black people have not been stopped in their
search for freedom and their affirmation of an identity.

The Afro-Uruguayan woman writer's preoccupation with identity and resistance is a thematic constant that is prevalent in the poems of Cledia Núñez Altamiranda and Cristina Rodríguez Cabral. "Canto negro" (poema en 3 cantos) / "Black Song" (poem in 3 chants) by Altamiranda begins with an idyllic description of Africa and ends with an exhortation to blacks to fight for their freedom, as is evident in the first "Song":

> Canto que llega del fondo
> de las selvas africanas.
> Canto que canto
>   Nostalgia y llanto
> Manos batiendo los parches
>   Negros bailando
> Plenilunio que refleja,
> Palmeras en lontananza
>   Canto con voz de esperanza
> Que en la selva resonó.
> Venus negra que soñaste
> Romance en la noche blanca.
> Blanca como la ilusión.
> Raza fuerte, vigorosa
> de la selva esplendorosa
> eras la dueña y señora.
> Pero tu gran poderío
> Y el fulgor de los tesoros
> que el Africa poseía
> habrían de ser el imán
> que a tus costas llevaría
> al traficante ambicioso
> que destrozara tu hogar.[18]

> [Song which arrives from the depth
> of the African jungles.
> Song that I sing
>   Nostalgia and scream
> Hands playing drums
>   Blacks dancing
> Full moon which reflects
> Palm trees in the background
>   I sing with a voice of hope
> Which resounded in the jungle.
> Black Venus who dreamed of
> Poetry in the white night.

White like the illusion.
Strong race, vigorous
from the splendid jungle
you are the owner and proprietess.
But your great power
And the splendor of the treasures
that Africa possessed
would have to be the magnet
which to your coasts would bring
the ambitious trafficker
who destroyed your home.'

The first "Song" sings of African origins, of harmony between humans and the natural environment. In this semiparadise from the poetic perspective, Blacks were in charge of their own destiny: "Strong race . . . owner and proprietess," but this would be disrupted by the "ambitious trafficker/who destroyed your home." "Song I" thus ends on an ominous note, which is amplified in the second chant:

Y el chocar de las olas
Contra el barco negrero
Amortigua los ecos
del TAMTAM tamborero.
Y el llanto nubló los ojos
de todas las madres negras.
El negro fue trasplantado
Y su cuerpo lacerado.
¡Ay el Africa lejana
Ay la selva esplendorosa!
    La luna no fue tan blanca.
Y en la noche oscura de su pensamiento
El negro llora su futuro incierto
Dolor de raza fuerte escarnecida
que desde lo más hondo de su pobre vida
gestaba la rebelión.
Y ese grito tan ansiado
llegarían sin tardanza.
América fue la esperanza
de Ayer, de Hoy, de Mañana.

                                        (58)

[And the collision of the waves
Against the slaveship
Softens the echoes

of the TAMTAM drummer.
And the cry clouded the eyes
of all the black mothers.
The black man was transplanted
And his body lacerated
Ah far away Africa!
Ah the splendid jungle!
    The moon was not so white
And in the dark night of your thought
The black man weeps an uncertain future
Pain of a strong race ridiculed
which from the very depths of its poor life
generated rebellion.
And the long-awaited cry
would arrive without delay
America was the hope
of Yesterday, Today and Tomorrow.]

The slave ship is placed in ironic juxtaposition to the paradaisal vision of Africa articulated in the first stanza. The waves mimic the drum while the white moon darkens, another symbolic contrast. The physical and mental anguish associated with displacement and uncertainty about the future is highlighted through images of dislocation and displacement. But these adverse conditions "generated rebellion," which assures the future of black people in societies that try to deny their existence.

"Song III" is an open exhortation of black freedom and progress:

¡¡Libertad!!
¡Y sonaron las trompetas!
Se encendieron las antorchas
De la libertad soñada.
Ya los cinco continentes
Ese grito estremeció.
Y hoy el negro se levanta
desde el fondo de los tiempos
Y es promesa de esperanza, canto de fe
Y otros hombres de otras razas
que ayer al negro envolvieron
    con el látigo infamante,
    ¡le rinden admiración!
Hermano negro que luchas
por la conquista social
más grande del Universo. ¡Tu libertad!

Sigue siempre cuesta arriba
No des vuelta la cabeza
Ni te detengas, ¡jamás!
Que la jornada es muy dura,
Y si luchas, ¡vencerás!
Y cuando llegue la hora,
    En el crisol que se funden
    Los Ideales más puros,
    ¡Las razas se fundirán!!
                (59)

[Freedom!
And the trumpets sounded!
They lit the torches
Of dreamed freedom.
Now five continents
Trembled with that cry.
And today the black man rises up
from the depths of time
And it is a promise of hope, song of faith
And other men of other races
who yesterday encircled the black man
    with the infamous whip
    extend admiration to him!
Black brother who fights
for the greatest social gain
of the Universe. Your freedom!
Always continue uphill
Don't look back
Don't stop, never!
The task is very hard
And if you fight, you will win!
And when the time arrives,
    In the crucible where are distilled
    The purest Ideals
    The races will merge!]

Out of this struggle and resistance to domination, respect for black people will be earned. And what will be gained by this push for equality? Idealistically the poetic voice surmises: "The purest ideals/The races will merge!" The idea of a melting pot is problematic because in the scenario of miscegenation, blacks will be asked to subordinate their hard-earned identity. These three "chants" interpret the black experience from imprisonment and slavery to freedom, self-affirmation, and equality.

The issues of resistance and liberation are addressed in two poems by Cristina Rodríguez Cabral (1959–): "Monte-vi-deo" and "Memoria y Resistencia"/"Memory and Resistance." The former poem explores the urban context:

> Ciudad que me ha visto nacer, crecer
> > amar, sufrir
> > > morir
> > > y hasta resucitar
> hoy me mira con ojos extraños
> me señala con su tradicional
> > > dedo crítico
> y me condena al exilio.
> ¿Por qué has olvidado
> tu antigua sonrisa
> de niña mimada
> asomándose a la vida?;
> el horror, la angustia
> y el aislamiento
> no han de ser obstáculos suficientes
> como para impedirnos
> defender
> cada pétalo
> de tu murguera flor.[19]

> [City that has seen me born, grow up
> > love, suffer
> > > die
> > > and even resuscitated
> today looks at me with foreign eyes
> points me out with its traditional
> > > critical finger
> and condemns me to exile.
> Why have you forgotten
> your ancient smile
> of a pampered child
> beginning to show life?
> the horror, the anguish
> the isolation
> they don't have to be sufficient obstacles
> to impede us from
> defending
> each petal
> of your withering flower.]

"Monte-vi-deo" is a poem of rejection from the perspective of an alienated black subject. The implicit question is, "Why us, if we have been such an integral part of your being?" But the isolation, the inner exile, the past atrocities are not enough to impede the protagonist from resisting marginalization. "Monte-vi-deo" is a poem of social and spiritual isolation. The poetic voice views itself as an orphan in an insensitive society that sees no positive value in the existence of Afro-Uruguayans. The sense of exile is internal, within, and represents the impact of psychological distance between the individual and the maternal archetypal center. But as Culler points out, "groups may make identities imposed on them into resources for that group" (118). In this instance, the speaker converts the negative experience of Afro-Uruguayans into a positive mode for change.

It is precisely in "Memory and Resistance" that the postcolonial processes of abrogation and appropriation are best exemplified from the perspective of the speaker. Framed within the dialectical tension between a black man and woman, the female voice demands respect, recognition, and her place in history as well. Through an extended apostrophe, she reminds him:

> Soy resistencia y memoria.
> Construí el camino del amo
> así como el de la libertad.
> Morí en la Casa Grande
> igual que en la Senzala.
> Dejé el ingenio y descalza
> me hice cimarrona.
> Sola fui comunidad, casa y gobierno
> porque escasas veces estuviste allí;
> Hombre Negro sin memoria,
> codo a codo
> espalda contra espalda,
> sigues sin estar allí.[20]

> [I am resistence and memory.
> I built the owner's road
> like the one of freedom.
> I died in the Big House
> same as in the Field.
> I left the sugar mill and
> became a cimarron.
> Alone I was community, home and government

because very seldom were you there
Black Man without memory
shoulder to shoulder
back to back
you continue without being here.]

This poem is a fervent call for respect and recognition by the black woman. The irony here is that her ire is directed toward the black man, who is also unempowered and not capable of improving her situation materially. The point the speaker is making, however, is that historically the black woman has been the lowest of the low and afforded little historical significance. By alluding to Gilberto Freyre's classic work of slave culture (*Casa Grande/Senzala*), the speaker makes the point that the exploitation of women was multifaceted. The black man is guilty of both *forgetting* her role in his survival and not acknowledging her presence, therefore not affording her the proper respect. This poem is a reminder to him to face reality:

Negro,
nuestro ausente de siempre,
generación tras generación,
yo te parí,
como a tu padre
y a tus hermanos.
Yo curvé la espalda
sujetándote durante la cosecha;
sangro, lucho, resisto
y desconoces mi voz.
ausente en tus memorias
y hallada culpable
vivo
prisionera del tiempo
y del estereotipo.
Fueron mis senos
quienes te alimentaron,
y al hijo del amo también
Fuí sangre mezclada en el barro
con látigo, humillaciones
y el estupro después.
Desde allí desplegué
al viento mis alas;
madre,
    negra,
        cimarrona,

Iemanjá,
Oxum,
        e Iansá a la vez.

[Black man,
our absent one of always,
generation after generation
I birthed you,
the same as your father
and your brothers.
I bent my back
steadying you during the harvest;
I bleed, fight, resist
and you ignore my voice.
absent in your memories
and found guilty
I live
prisoner of time
and of the stereotype.
Those were my breasts
that nourished you,
and the owner's son also
I was blood mixed in the clay
with a whip, humiliations
and rape afterward.
from there I spread
my wings to the wind;
mother,
    black,
            maroon
Iemanjá,
Oxum,
        and Iansá at the same time.]

The mother figure is appropriately defined in relation to goddesses
of water—symbolizing life and creation—of the Yoruba pantheon: Iemanjá, (sea/mother of all Orishas), Oxum (fresh water/gold), and
Iansá (Candombe/wind and storms).

Black womanhood is elevated to an archetypal level as origin and
mother, as a solitary and sustaining figure through labor, sustenance,
suffering, violation, and above all resistance to oblivion. Out of this
historical struggle emerges a persona solidly grounded in historical
reality and religion consciousness.

The overall theme of the poem is cultural maroonage as manifested in the mother figure who conserves not just black ancestral

memory but is also a repository of contemporary values. Identity is addressed within the contexts of femininity and miscegenation. Anaphora with "yo"/ "I" is a powerful affirmation of this concept:

> Yo,
> memoria perdida
> que atraviesa tus ventanas,
> yo,
> piel azabache y manos raídas.
> Yo,
> Negra;
> Yo,
> Mestiza
> corazón tibio y desnudos pies.
> Yo
> traje raído y pelo salvaje,
> yo con mis labios gruesos
> te proclamé rey.
> Yo,
> compañera de lucha y de sueños
> a quien tu ausencia y la vida
> le enseñaron
> le exigieron
> mucho más que a calentar
> tu pan
> y tu almohada.
>
> (104–5)

> [I,
> lost memory
> that passes by your windows,
> I,
> black skin and callused hands,
> I,
> Black;
> I,
> Mestiza
> a warm heart and bare feet
> I
> torn clothes and disheveled hair
> with my thick lips
> pronounced you king.
> I,
> companion of battle and dreams
> to whom your absence and life

showed
demanded
much more than warming
your bread
and your pillow.]

The speaker's unwavering presence is juxatposed to his glaring absence as a positive manifestation and affirmation of black culture. The tendency of some blacks to look to "improve the race" by seeking unions with whites or somebody lighter on the color spectrum is foregrounded in this tense assessment of male/female relations. In the final analysis, the speaker demands respect on her own terms while providing a memory refreshing history lesson at the same time.

Cristina Rodríguez Cabral, and her Afro-Uruguayan predecessors have developed a counterdiscourse, based upon the rhetoric of identity, demanding that their legitimacy as Afro-Uruguayans be recognized. If there is one motif that unifies the themes of identity and resistance in Afro-Uruguayan poetry, it is orphanhood. The sense of loss and abandonment expressed in these works is based upon historical circumstances, based upon the exile and exploitation of blacks in the Americas, to which the writers bear witness. In their process of black subject construction, Afro-Uruguayan poets are answering the call for self-affirmation, issued by Timoteo Olivera in 1872.

5

Jorge Emilio Cardoso
and the Afro-Uruguayan Dramatic Tradition

Jorge Emilio Cardoso (1938–), the most successful contemporary black dramatist, stands on the shoulders of a number of Afro-Uruguayan playwrights who have sought to make the genre an integral component of Uruguayan culture. The pages of black journals of the early decades of the century are replete with efforts by dramatists to make their works known to the public.

In its first number, published in 1939, *Renovación/Renewal,* the cultural journal, issued a call for Afro-Uruguayans to revive their theatrical tradition, exhorting them in the following manner:

> *Renovación,* con el optimismo característico que ostentaremos, espera que dentro de poco se organicen nuestros aficionados y vuelvan a brindarnos las veladas artísticas de tan feliz memoria como las del "Colón" y el "Albéniz" . . . Brindamos a nuestros lectores el "cliché" de la figura tan destacada de nuestro teatro, la señorita Zenona Suárez Peña.[1]

> [*Renovación* with the characteristic optimism that we show off, hopes that soon our followers will organize and again provide us the artistic evenings with such happy memories as those of the "Colón" and the "Albéniz" . . . We extend to our readers the "cliché" of the most outstanding figure of our theater, Ms. Zenona Suárez Peña.]

Renovación devoted a regular column to "Nuestro Teatro"/"Our Theatre" in which it sought to contextualize Afro-Uruguayan dramatic production: "Theatre patrons have to fight in our environment with many difficulties: of an economic and technical nature." This has been the reality of Afro-Uruguayan theater from its inception to the present. Undaunted by the obstacles, *Renovación* continued to render homage to the pioneers, Abel Cardozo in particular, who: "Cumplió las bodas de plata en nuestros escenarios, pues debutó en el 'Almas que luchan', que dirigiera con acierto D. Victor Ocampo Vilaza, y continuó en escala ascendente hasta dirigir él varios cuadros de aficionados"[2] ["Celebrated his silver anniversary on our stages, since he debuted in 'Souls that Fight,' which D. Victor Ocampo Vilaza directed skillfully and continued on an upward trajectory until he directed several popular scenes"]. Abel Cardozo was an outstanding actor and director in the evolution of early black theater in Uruguay.

Carlos Cardozo Ferreira and Roberto Cisnero, two of the preeminent Afro-Uruguayan poets of the 1930s and '40s, were also involved in black theater. In July 1942, *Nuestra Raza* announced that "The brothers Ofir and C. Cardozo Ferreira, will stage a theatrical work." It goes on to state:

> "Amor y prejuicios." Esta obra en un prólogo y tres actos es de ambiente estudiantil y su trama gira en torno al cristianismo como factor de libertad de los pueblos y de los prejuicios de raza. Dirigirá la escenificación el veterano director conrazáneo José Pedro Cardozo.[3]

> ["Love and Prejudice." This work in a prologue and three acts has a student environment and its plot revolves around Christianity as a liberating factor of people and racial prejudices. The production will be staged by the veteran black director José Pedro Cardozo.]

Although there was no follow-up regarding the success or failure of this dramatic presentation, Cardozo Ferreira remained a positive force on the artistic scene for decades, as documented in the black press.

Roberto Cisnero published *Candombe sckech* [sic], one of the few Afro-Uruguayan dramas to appear in print in its entirety. "Candombe," a two-page dramatic interlude, set in the Barrio Sur, uses the music of the "Candombe Oriental" as a backdrop for resolving issues of racism and cultural insensitivity. Cisnero's work, "El Vagabundo"/"The Vagabond," was also staged in the Teatro Albéniz as a benefit for *Nuestra Raza*.[4] These pioneering efforts by Cardozo Ferreira and Cisnero were advanced further by César Techera and José Isabelino Gares.

"Candombe," the play by Cisnero, externalizes and synthesizes many of the prejudicial attitudes held against blacks in Uruguay. This brief one scene encounter transpires between Mabel and Pepe, a couple, on a balcony in the Barrio Sur. He cannot understand why she has changed the manner in which their relationship is developing. It seems as if Mabel's perception of the world has changed, especially as it relates to black people. She explains:

> Hoy pienso, y razono humanamente. Antes, no; es que vivía en un mundo ilusionado, en un mundo donde nos creíamos superior a otros seres . . . Creando entonces ese prejuicio racial, que tanto mal hace al mundo, a este mundo que hoy llamamos civilizado.[5]

> [Today I think and reason humanly. Before, no; it is that I lived in an illusioned world, in a world where we believed ourselves superior to other beings . . . Creating therefore that racial prejudice, which does so much evil to the world, to this world which today we call civilized.]

This change has come about, miraculously, due to music but Pepe is not convinced. The following exchange occurs:

Pepe.   ¡Bah! Música de negros, música de salvajes . . .
Mabel. ¡No . . . ! Música humana . . . Música que lleva en sí todo el dolor . . . O toda su alegría . . . según lo sienta y les dicte sus corazones.
Pepe.   ¿Un negro que piense? ¿Un negro que siente? . . . ¡Bah! Me hace gracia. Mira Mabel, el negro nació esclavo, y su signo es servir, trabajar en el campo . . . lustrar los zapatos . . . lavar los pisos . . . ser soldado . . . y a lo sumo-portero de oficina del Estado, y creo que para eso no se necesita mucha inteligencia, si la tuviera, desde luego.
Mabel. Pepe, te prohibo que hables así. (17)

[Pepe.   Bah! Music of blacks, music of savages . . .
Mabel. No . . . ! Human music . . . Music which carries with it all of the pain . . . Or all of its happiness . . . according to how one feels and what the heart dictates.
Pepe.   A black who thinks? A black who feels? . . . Bah! That's funny. Look, Mabel, the black was born a slave, and his destiny is to serve, work in the field, shine shoes . . . scrub floors . . . be a soldier . . . and at the most—doorman of a state office, and I believe for that much intelligence is not necessary, even if he had it, by the way.
Mabel. Pepe, I forbid you to say that.]

Pepe articulates many of the basic stereotypes associated with the origin and destiny of Afro-Uruguayans that have persisted until this day. He builds upon one of the basic dichotomies in the literature in the Southern Cone—civilization versus barbarism. The dialectical process at work in this scene allows Mabel to speak of "civilized" in an ironic fashion while Pepe is convinced of the "savage" nature of blacks. Mabel counters with the idea of one human race and elaborates a list of achievers from the African diaspora, from Argentina and Paraguay to Brazil to Cuba to the United States. Ultimately, Pepe acknowledges his ignorance and the "sketch" ends on a positive note. The importance of a seemingly minor piece such as this is that since its inception black drama in Uruguay has served to educate the public and to combat ignorance and racism. Since the audience to which this piece is directed is black, the objective is to foster ethnic pride.

César A. Techera was an actor and dramatist from Rocha who enjoyed unprecedented success on the Montevideo theatrical scene. His major accomplishments are summarized in the following manner:

> Más tarde con la colaboración de otros jóvenes artistas crea la Agrupación Cultural y Teatral "Florencio Sánchez,"—de cuya entidad, además de ser el "alma mates,"—su actuación como actor, fue todo un éxito habiendo conquistado sinceras simpatías y aplausos a través de toda la cadena de "Teatro de Barrio" y Teatros de Verano . . . su mayor conquista artística fue al formarse la Comedia Nacional.[6]

> [Later with the collaboration of other young artists he creates the Agrupación Cultural y Teatral "Florencio Sánchez,"—an entity, in addition to being the heart and soul,—his performance as actor, was a success having conquered sincere feelings and applause throughout the chain of "Teatro de Barrio" and Teatros de Verano . . . his greatest artistic achievement was forming the Comedia Nacional.]

During 1948, for example, the Florencio Sánchez theatrical group, under the direction of Techera, presented plays by its namesake, and also by González Pacheco, Bidart Zansi, and Pirandello, and was recognized as one of the leading companies in Uruguay. As documented in the black press, Techera enjoyed a long and distinguished career as administrator, director and actor.

Another major figure in the evolution of the Afro-Uruguayan dramatic tradition was José Isabelino Gares (1872–1940), also known as Isabelino José Gares, whose authored works such as "Almas que luchan"/"Souls that Fight" (1912), "El carancho"/"The Owl" (1924), "Los Tordos"/"The Starlings" (1928), "Mis blasones"/"My Coat of Arms" (1930), and *El camino de la redención/The Road to Redemption* (1931). Many of Gares's works were performed in the Teatro Colón.[7] "La vorágine: la despoblación de la raza negra en los departamentos de campaña"/"The Vortex: The Depopulation of the Black Race in the Departments of the Campaign," Gares's other major work of the period, was also the topic of discussion in *Nuestra Raza*.[8]

He became the dominant figure of the Afro-Uruguayan theatrical scene in its early evolution and was one of the leading intellectuals of his time.[9] In addition to being the premier dramatist, Gares was also an accomplished poet and essayist. Most of his scholarly output was afrocentric, that is, devoted to making others aware of the importance of Afro-Uruguayan contributions to the culture. Toward that end, Gares authored an important essay entitled "Contribución al Estudio de la Participación de la Raza Negra a la Formación de la Democracia en América"/"Contributions to the Study of the Participation of the Black Race to the Formation of Democracy in America." Excerpts of this insightful piece were included in *Acción*, 1, 12 (30 March 1935): 3.

Gares also addressed the issue of Afro-Uruguayan cultural maintenance in an essay, "Los Escritores y la Raza Negra"/"Writers and the Black Race." Regarding the African heritage, Gares states:

> En este país hace casi medio siglo que desaparecieran del ambiente los locales donde se bailaban el candombe, las naciones "Congas," "Banguelas" y los "Magi" de cuyos atávicos ritos y costumbres no han quedado rastros.[10]

> [In this country it has almost been half a century since the disappearance of the sites where the "Congas," "Banguelas" and the "Magi" nations danced the Candombe and of whose atavistic rites and customs not a trace remains.]

Gares's position was that since so much of Afro-Uruguayan culture has been lost, there is an urgent necessity to reclaim its remnants. Gares was convinced that the future of Afro-Uruguayans would be more meaningful if they understood the past better. Regarding the lack of concrete remnants of African culture, Gares surmises:

> Esto no quiere decir en manera alguna, que desconozcamos o neguemos nuestro origen africano, del que orgullosos nos com-

placemos, sino, es que hemos ido avanzando al ritmo del progreso, prosperando en las diversas manifestaciones de la cultura de nuestro país. (2).

[This does not mean in any way that we do not know about or deny our African origin, which fills us with pride, rather we have been advancing to the rhythm of progress, prospering in the diverse manifestations of the culture of our country.]

Ultimately, Gares's view is assimiliationist, a route that most Afro-Uruguayans have sought to follow.

As a journalist, Gares served on the editorial board of *La Vanguardia/Vanguard* during its second era, which began on 15 January 1928. He was the secretary of publication and also edited the regular column entitled "Nuestro Teatro"/ "Our Theatre," which kept the reading public abreast of Afro-Uruguayan theatrical activity throughout the country. The column included reviews of performances as well as interviews with actors and directors. As a dramatist, Gares left very little of his own work in the public domain. In response to the question of Daniel Braquet in the journal *Paula* regarding the relationship between Gares's works and mainstream Uruguayan theater, Juanamaría Cordones-Cook responded: "sus obras no perduraran. La única editada fue *El camino de la redención* de la cual solo su familia conserva un ejemplar junto a los manuscritos del resto de su producción teatral"[11] ["his works did not last. The only published one was *The Road to Redemption* of which only his family retains a copy along with the manuscripts of the rest of his theatrical production"]. In fact, *Los Tordos* was also published in 1928. The advertisement read: "Apareció *Los Tordos* del conocido autor Isabelino José Gares que acaba de estrenarse con éxito por el cuadro 'Nobleza gaucha' en la Casa del Arte"[12] ["*The Starlings* appeared by the known author Isabelino José Gares who just presented with success the play 'Gaucho Nobility' in the Casa del Arte"]. Subsequent praise for *Los Tordos/The Starlings* and its publication appeared in the next number of *La Vanguardia.*

Judging by the contemporaneous reactions that appeared in the black press regarding his works, Gares was admired and appreciated by his peers. In a brief homage rendered to Gares on his death, entitled: "José I. Gares, Poeta y Dramaturgo de Color"/ "José I. Gares, Poet and Dramaturg of Color," Isidoro Casas Pereyra comments briefly on two of the dramatist's works directed by Ignacio Suárez

Peña. They are *The Starlings* ("un boceto donde el sentimiento y el humorismo estaban bien dilineados" ["a sketch where feelings and humor were well defined] and *A Stop in the Road* ("teatro estilo sanchista, copia fiel de esa vida de gente de condición social reducida" ["Sánchez-style theater, a true copy of the life of people from poor social conditions"]. Casas Pereyra's final assessment of Gares was "su dialogada ágil y su concepción teatral era bastante firme y que por momentos lograba impresionar"[13] ["his agile dialogue and his dramatic conception were very solid and sometimes were impressive"].

El camino de la redención/The Road to Redemption (1931) is Isabelino José Gares's major published work. Subtitled: *Ensayo de Comedia Racial en Dos Actos/Essay of Racial Comedy in Two Acts*, this drama addresses many of the issues and concerns prevalent in the Afro-Uruguayan community. Ethnicity, class structure, economics, and racism are foregrounded in this look at a black family striving to progress in Uruguayan society. Within this context, honor emerges as a primary thematic motif. This two-act drama was first performed on stage at the Teatro Albéniz in Montevideo on October 5, 1935.

In "Dos Palabras"/"Two Words," the preface to his drama, Gares makes clear that his intention is not to divide, but rather to create harmony and understanding among blacks and whites in Montevideo. He states:

> Está remotamente lejos de nuestro ánimo pretender despertar irrisorios odios de razas que felizmente, no se han arraigado, ni se arraigarán jamás en el culto país de Artigas y Rodó; reeditando entre nosotros los lamentables e inferiorizantes espectáculos los que constituyen su secuela y repugnan a los sentimientos humanos que orientan nuestras modalidades sociales. Más lejos aún de nuestras aspiraciones la absurda pretensión de querer correr una línea divisoria entre el Teatro que tuvo por precursor a Florencio Sánchez, el más grande dramaturgo de la América Latina y nuestros incipientes ensayos de teatro negro, sino dar forma viva, expresión palpitante a nuestras inquietudes y a los inherentes problemas y sentimientos de puro sabor racial.[14]

> [It is remotely far from our spirit to pretend to awaken ridiculous race hatred which happily, have not been rooted, nor will they ever be rooted in the sophisticated country of Artigas and Rodó; reinitiating amongst us the lamentable and demeaning spectacles that constitute its consequence and disgust the human feelings that guide our social mores. Even further from our aspirations is the absurd pretention of wishing to drive a divisive wedge between the theatre

which had Florencio Sánchez, the greatest dramatist in Latin America, as precursor and our newly founded rehearsals of black theater, rather to give live form, pulsating expressoin to our uncertainties and to our innate problems and feelings of pure racial flavor.]

Often, however the stated intentions of a writer and the final outcome of his work do not coincide. While *The Road to Redemption* does not overtly condemn black-white relationships, the play's worldview calls into question many societal assumptions based upon ethnicity. In his preliminary "Juicio"/"Judgment" of the work, Ildefonso Pereda Valdés refers to it as "un interesante ensayo de comedia dramática de carácter racial" ["an interesting work of dramatic comedy of racial character"] (9). Pereda Valdés compares *The Road to Redemption* to *Our Children* by Florencio Sánchez and concludes:

"El Camino de la Redención" es en resúmen una obra que se hacía esperar en el ambiente de color, pues, era ya tiempo que los escritores de la raza en el Uruguay enfocaran sus trabajos literarios sobre temas raciales y trataran de ofrecernos algunos ensayos sobre la psicología de su raza. (p. 10)

["The Road to Redemption" is in sum a work which had been anticipated amongst the coloreds, well, it was about time that writers of the race in Uruguay focused their literary works upon racial themes and tried to offer us some observations about the psychology of their race.]

These inspirational comments by Pereda Valdés, expressing the need to incorporate ethnic concerns, were taken to heart by Gares and his generation because the decades of the thirties and forties in Uruguay yielded more sustained quality creative activity than any period until the recent burgeoning of Afro-Uruguayan cultural affirmation.

The Road to Redemption is about discrimination, on the job and in personal relationships. The play interprets the reality of the family of Marcelo and Hermina, who are the parents of Ernesto and Lucía. Marcelo confronts prejudice at work, while Lucía deals with the same phenomenon in the person of Federico, her lover.

Externally, *The Road to Redemption* is divided into two acts: the first with sixteen scenes and the second thirteen. The seven primary characters cover the color spectrum: "moreno(-a)" "dark," "parda casi oscura"/"brown almost dark," "Mulata"/"mulatto," and "de cutis blanco"/"with white skin." Only Ernesto, the son of Herminia and Marcelo and the brother of Lucía is presented without a description of his color. Federico, the white character, and Lucía's lover, is portrayed in antagonistic fashion throughout the play.

The first act begins its evolution in an unspectacular fashion in the dining room of a "poor house," where Lucía is ironing, Herminia is knitting, and Carmen is gossiping. The dramatic tension inherent in the exposition gradually increases and reaches its climax in the closing scenes as Lucía confronts Federico about assuming the responsibility for her pregnancy. The author uses dramatic irony to create suspicion about Lucía's physical and mental states in the initial scene when Carmen reminds Herminia that "appearances deceive" and raises the issue of class in the relationship. The exchange occurs as follows:

D. Carmen.	(Algo nerviosa) Digo . . . para no darle motivo a esas y otras malas lenguas . . . vamos . . . bien podría buscar otro novio que . . . (Buscando la palabra) que . . . fuera . . . vamos, de su misma categoría . . . es decir, de su misma clase como se dice . . .
D. Herminia.	(Silencio). ¿Y esa es la causa para que hablen?
D. Carmen.	Creo que no es mal muchacho . . . (Con tono de adulación). ¡Y la pobre Lucía muy buena! . . . ¡Dios me libre ofenderlos! . . .
D. Herminia.	(Como consigo misma) ¡Dichoso novio! . . . (Como quien toma una resolución) Mire . . . en cuanto vea la madre de esas haraganas se lo diré . . . vaya si se lo diré, pierda usted cuidado, va a ver cómo les va a ir . . .

[D. Carmen.	(A bit nervous) I say . . . In order not to give a motive to those and other evil tongues . . . well . . . you could very well find another boyfriend who . . . (searching for the word) who were well, of your same group . . . that is to say, of your same class as they say . . .
D. Herminia.	(Silence). And that is the reason why they talk?
D. Carmen.	I believe he is not a bad fellow . . . (With a tone of praise) And poor Lucía so good! God forgive me for offending them!
D. Herminia.	(As if to herself) Lucky fiancé! . . . (Like somebody making a resolution) Look . . . as soon as I see the mothers of those bums I will say it . . . Go ahead if you want to say it, throw caution to the wind, it's going to be how you tell them . . .]

This relationship between Lucía and Federico is doomed to fail due to issues of class, color, and the negative attitude of Marcelo, Lucía's father. Herminia states: "Lucía, sabes bien que no soy yo quien se opone a esos amoríos tuyos, es tu padre. La verdad es que, desde que tienes esos amores, en esta casa no hay paz" ["Lucía, you know very well that I am not the one who opposes your love affairs it is your father. The truth is since you have had those affairs, there is no peace in the house"] (23).

Marcelo is a strong father figure who is feared and respected by his family. Outside of that domain, however, he has little influence and is devastated when he is passed over for a job. The bad news is announced to Marcelo by Ernesto, his son:

D. Marcelo.	Me habían dicho que la próximo semana.
Ernesto.	(Buscando el diario que ha traido. Silencio.) A ver . . . por aquí está . . . (Leyendo.) "Nombramientos de hoy" . . . aquí . . . "Debiéndose proveer el cargo de archivero . . . de la oficina . . . bueno . . .
D. Marcelo.	(Se ha puesto de pie visiblemente nervioso.) Sí . . . Sí. (Pausa).
Ernesto.	Se nombró al señor Agapito Aguerre.
D. Marcelo.	(Le arrebata el diario y lee en silencio. Paulatinamente irá bajando el diario y se sentará vencido.) Sí . . . sí . . . (Pausa). ¡Sí! . . . ¡No vé! (En voz baja). ¡El mismo que me habían dicho que tenía ambiente! (Silencio.)
Ernesto.	¿Y quién es ese señor?
D. Marcelo.	Creo que un señorito de no sé qué Comité . . .
Ernesto.	(Interrumpiendo un nuevo silencio.) Y bueno papá, hay que tener paciencia . . .
D. Marcelo.	(Como consigo mismo.) ¡Hay que tener paciencia! . . . ¡Hay que tener paciencia! . . . ¡Más todavía! . . . (Transición.) ¡Sea uno bueno, más bueno de lo que tiene obligación de ser un hombre. Soporte esa perra vida hasta de correveidile . . . ¡Sofrene el potro de la dignidad, alimente día a día la planta de la esperanza! . . . ¿Para qué? ¡Para que cuando llegue el momento de hacerle a una justicia, se olvidan de un hombre que se entregó, todo él, toda su fé! . . . ¡Antigüedad! . . . ¡Competencia! . . . ¡Por qué! ¡Para qué! (Silencio.)
Ernesto.	(Un algo abismado.) No creí papá, que iba a causarle disgusto . . .

D. Marcelo.   (Interrumpiendo.) Este trago amargo! . . . La absoluta
confianza que he tenido y aún sigo teniendo en mis señ-
ores jefes. Y en esta emergencia creía una seguridad . . .
que no llego a comprender yo mismo . . . (31–32)

[D. Marcelo. They had told me next week.

Ernesto.   (Looking for the newspaper he had brought. Silence.)
Let's see . . . here it is . . . (Reading.) "Today's appoint-
ments" . . . here . . . "Having to provide the position of
archiver . . . of the office" . . . well . . .

D. Marcelo.   (He has stood up, visibly nervous.) Yes . . . Yes . . . (Pause).

Ernesto.   They named Mr. Agapito Aguerre.

D. Marcelo.   (He snatches the paper and reads in silence. He will
slowly lower the paper and sits down, defeated.) Yes . . .
yes . . . (Pause.) Yes! . . . Don't you see? (In a low voice.)
The same one who told me he was content! (Silence.)

Ernesto.   And who is that man?

D. Marcelo.   I believe he is a little guy from who knows what committee . . .

Ernesto.   (Interrupting a new silence.) And well, poppa, one must
have patience . . .

D. Marcelo.   (As to himself.) One must be patient! . . . One must be
patient! . . . Even more! (Transition.) Let me be good,
better than a man is obligated to be. Bear this bitch of a
life like a fairy tale. Rein in the colts of dignity, nurture
daily the plant of hope! . . . For what reason? So that
when the moment comes to do him justice, they forget a
man who gave of himself, everything, all of his faith! . . .
Longevity! . . . Competence! . . . Why? For what reason?
(Silence.)

Ernesto.   (A bit amazed.) I didn't think, poppa, it would cause you
such anger . . .

D. Marcelo.   (Interrupting.) This bitter pill . . . The absolute confi-
dence I have had and continue having in my bosses. And
in this emergency believed in security . . . that I myself am
unable to comprehend.]

Marcelo's initial reaction to the fact that he is not rewarded with
the position he deserved is one of dismay. Marcelo does not understand, initially, that in spite of his loyalty, longevity, competence, and
trust in his superiors, another factor in his promotion, color, is even
more important. It is later, in a pivotal scene with Lucía, that Marcelo
faces the truth of his situation:

(Consigo mismo.) ¡Haber nacido pobre, resignado a trabajar toda la vida, es decir a ser mandado y respetar! . . . ¡Nombrese a Don Agapito Aguerre! . . . (Sarcástico, rie.) ¡Ja, ja, ja! . . . Veinticinco años de servicios! ¿Para qué? . . . (Pausa. Por el cutis de su mano.) ¡Esto, nada más que esto! . . . (En voz baja irá excitándose paulatinamente.) ¿No somos todos los hombres iguales? No nacemos del mismo barro? Con los mismos sentimientos, las mismas alegrías, los mismos dolores! . . . ¿Y no vamos al foso de la misma tierra, para podrirnos y ser festín de los gusanos? . . . (Silencio. Levanta la vista y parece sorprenderse por la presencia de Lucía.) ¿Cómo, estabas vos aquí? . . . (35)

[To himself.) To have been born poor, resigned to working all of one's life, that is to say to be commanded and respected . . . Don Agapito Aguerre was named! . . . (Sarcastic laugh.) Ha, ha, ha! . . . Twenty-five years of service! For what? . . . (Pause. Looks at the skin of his hand.) This, no more than this! . . . (In a low voice gradually getting excited.) Aren't all men equal? Aren't we born of the same clay? With the same feelings, the same happiness, the same pain? And don't we go into a hole in the same earth, to rot and be a feast for worms! . . . (Silence. He glances up and seems surprised by the presence of Lucía.) What, you were here?

At his most agonizing climactic moment, Marcelo still does not wish to openly acknowledge that racism is the reason he is not promoted. "This, nothing more than this!" is Marcelo's reaction after acknowledging his blackness. The existential questions he poses regarding common origins, equality, and destiny are rhetorical. Skin color, it seems, is the determining factor in Marcelo's particular inability to ascend the socioeconomic ladder.

This scene is indeed a climactic one in that not only does Marcelo recognize racism for what it is, but he also confronts Lucía about the legitimacy of her relationship with Federico. As a result, Lucía realizes that Federico does not share her feelings about their relationship. This is revealed in Lucía's final plea for Federico to accept his responsibility:

Lucía.   No comprendes que no puedo vivir más en esta angustiosa incertidumbre. (Sollozante.) Hace ya mucho tiempo que me prometes lo mismo y los días pasan . . .

Federico. (Malhumorado.) Y qué quieres, que robe? . . .

Lucía.   ¡Oh, ese no, Federico! Pero piensa que si lo que te pido es algún sacrificio, no olvides que ve ya lo hice primero por tí.

Federico. Y en recompensa me exiges lo que no puedo, y te crees que con reproches . . .

Lucía.   Con reproches, no; con tus promesas. Cuando hiciste presa mi cuerpo de tu voracidad de varón, me lo exigías como una prueba de amor.

Federico.   Ahora, te arrepientes y quieres justificarte.

Lucía.   No. Eso no. Quiero decirte que creí en tus palabras, en tu sinceridad, y en el momento que los hechos se precipitan creo que debes protegerme . . . escucharme . . .

Federico.   ¿Y te parece que te he escuchado poco? (Se siente un silbido.) Ves, me llaman, me voy . . .

Lucía.   (Vuelve a interponerse.) No, Federico . . . escúchame . . . te lo ruego.

Federico.   (Que la hace a un lado.) Déjame, hasta mañana o pasado. (Mutis. Por el foro.)

[Lucía.   Don't you understand that I can't live any longer in this painful uncertainty. (Sobbing.) For a long time you have promised me the same and the days go by.

Federico.   (Angry.) And what do you want, me to steal?

Lucía.   Oh, that no, Federico! But if you think that what I ask for is some kind of sacrifice, don't forget I did it first of all for you.

Federico.   And in return you demand that I do what I can't, and you believe that with insults . . .

Lucía.   With insults, no; with your promises. When you imprisoned my body with your male voracity, you demanded it as a proof of love.

Federico.   Now you repent and wish to justify yourself . . .

Lucía.   No. That, no. I want to say I believed in your words, in your sincerity, and at the moment when things escalate I believe you must protect me . . . listen to me . . .

Federico.   And you believe I have listened to you only a little? (He hears a whistle.) Look, they are calling me, I'm going . . .

Lucía.   (Tries to stop him.) No, Federico . . . listen to me . . . I beg you.

Federico.   (Pushes her aside.) Leave me, until tomorrow or the day after. (Exit. By the back of the stage.)]

Lucía mistakes sex for love and is slow to realize that Federico's commitment is nonexistent. This scene ends with her imploring him, to no avail, to do the right thing for their unborn child, as the first act ends. Skin color is also at the root of their failed relationship, just as it is the determining factor in her father's attempt to climb the economic ladder. It is Marcelo who finally forces Federico to agree to marry Lucía in an effort to protect the family honor. This idea is rejected by Lucía in the end and all parties involved are satisfied with the outcome as *The Road to Redemption* reaches its nonresolution.

The Road to Redemption is a play that raises the issue but does not provide a solution to the presence of pervasive racism in Uruguayan society. This phenomenon not only controls decisions in the workplace but is also a factor in the most personal of relationships. Gares's treatment of the topic is forceful, but not overdone. As a playwright, he presents the characters in their circumstances and leaves the interpretation to the reader/audience. Read in relation to Uruguayan social practices regarding blacks, however, the play brings to the forefront issues that have persisted to this day.

The Road to Redemption is a technically accomplished drama. Believable characters are presented through thoughts, actions, and the perceptions of others. Stage directions are well-done, as the settings are reflective of emotional states and the movements of characters are precise. The silences inscribed in the text accentuate the level of dramatic tension in the various scenes. Overall, this is a tightly woven drama that captures a bygone era whose concerns are very much those of the present and, more than likely, the future. Gares, as playwright and intellectual, kept issues of color and class at the forefront of the Afro-Uruguayan agenda. In so doing, he helped to lay the groundwork for the subsequent socially motivated activities of the next generation of thinkers and activists.

Later in the aforementioned interview in *Paula* with Braquet, Cordones-Cook responded to a question regarding the impact of the intellectuals affiliated with *Nuestra Raza*:

> Era una minoría un poco cerrada y elitista, y una vez que ellos desaparecieran se produjo un vacío cultural y creativo, hasta que en 1945 el Comité de Entidades Negras del Uruguay (C.E.N.U.) proyecta reavivar las actividades creando un grupo de Teatro Negro que aunque no llegó a materializarse dejaría su semilla. (15)

> [It was a bit closed and elitist minority, and once they disappeared a creative and cultural vacuum was produced until in 1945 the Committee of Black Entities of Uruguay (CENU) planned to revive activities creating a Black Theatre group and although it did not materialize would leave its seed.]

The Comité de Entidades Negras del Uruguay/Committee of Black Entities of Uruguay (CENU) referred to in the interview is probably the Círculo de Intelectuales, Artistas, Periodistas, y Escritores Negros/Circle of Black Intellectuals, Artists, Journalists and Writers (CIAPEN), which was founded in 1945. In an editorial assessing the effectiveness of CIAPEN five years after its founding, *Rumbos* makes the point that the organization was:

> integrado por el más valioso núcleo de capacidades—con que contaba en este momento nuestra colectividad—como sea: Roberto Cisnero, Pilar E. Barrios, Mario L. Montero, Washington Viera, Ramón Pereyra, Alberto N. Méndez, José R. Suárez, Virginia B. de Salas, Anselmo I. García, Pedro Ferreyras y otros.[15]

> [integrated by the most outstanding nucleus of capable individuals—which were present at that moment in our collectivity—such as: Roberto Cisnero, Pilar E. Barrios, Mario L. Montero, Washington Viera, Ramón Pereyra, Alberto N. Méndez, José R. Suárez, Viriginia B. de Salas, Anselmo I. García, Pedro Ferreyras and others.]

The point is, that between the reappearance of *Nuestra Raza* in 1933, which was published continuously until 1948, and the closure of *Acción* in 1952, there was not a void in Afro-Uruguayan leadership and cultural activity, due to the contributions of intellectuals like Isabelino José Gares and others. Their dramatic tradition is long and storied but often there has been a lack of economic resources and will to sustain it. Afro-Uruguayan theater transcended Candombe and Carnaval to address important social issues, as demonstrated by the enduring contributions of Cardozo Ferreira, Suárez, Techera, and Gares.

The Teatro Negro Independiente, run by white Uruguayans, met with the same fate as Afro-Uruguayan initiatives but for different reasons. Black theater patrons and writers looked to the stage for artistic and intellectual stimulation, rather than social uplift, as was the case with the Teatro Negro Independiente, which was founded by Francisco Merino. The importance of attitude toward Afro-Uruguayan culture in the failure of the latter movement is revealed to Juanamaría Cordones-Cook in an interview with Tomás Olivera Chirimini who "explicaba ese fenómeno indicando que el generoso y altruista esfuerzo de Merino estaba teñido de un paternalismo tan excesivo que no había creado incentivos que estimularan la iniciativa personal"[16] ["explained that phenomenon indicating that the generous and altruistic effort of Merino was tainted by a paternalism so excessive that had not created incentives that would stimulate personal initiative"]. Apparently a theatrical movement based upon Afro-Uruguayan superstititions and stereotypes did not have much appeal to the potential audience. The approach taken by Rafael Murillo Selva Rendón, the Honduran playwright, in *Loubavagu* (1997), his culturalist interpretation of the Garífuna, is the most effective model to assure grassroots involvement in popular theater.[17]

Afro-Uruguayan dramatists recognized early on that in order for their works to be successful, they had to transcend ethnicity. A theater directed solely toward the black masses was sure to fail because this was the group least capable of sustaining, financially and intellectually, the productions. Jorge Emilio Cardoso is the latest dramatist to provide culturally specific drama of wide appeal.

Jorge Emilio Cardoso has established himself as a first-rate poet and dramatist whose recent autobiography further attests to his creative abilities. In addition to having his works appear in the *Antología de poetas negros uruguayos/Anthology of Black Uruguayan Poets*, edited by Alberto Britos, Cardoso has self-published *Los horizontes de Calunga/ The Horizons of Calunga* (1992), a collection of poetry; *Cinco veinte/ 520* (1995), autobiographical prose; and has written and presented *El desalojo de la calle de los negros/Eviction on the Street of the Blacks* (1995), a very successful play. He is currently engaged in other theatrical activity while writing, according to Cardoso, the epic novel of the Afro-Uruguayan experience, from slavery to the present.

This ability of Cardoso to combine the black experience with the national and the international is what accounts, in part, for the phenomenal success of *Eviction on the Street of the Blacks*. Written in 1992, this play finally made it to the public three years later. In a letter to me dated 18 August 1992 while the work was in progress, Cardoso expressed skepticism about the future of his play:

Estamos haciendo esfuerzos—con la gente de ACSU—de representarla dignamente, iniciando otra etapa en el teatro vocacional negro del Uruguay. Sin embargo acá todo se hace cada vez más difícil por la desidia espiritual de mis compatriotas quienes dejan entrever cada vez más claramente sus carencias educacionales que se profundizan con el tiempo.[18]

[We are making plans—with the people of ACSU—to stage it with dignity, initiating another era in the black vocational theatre of Uruguay. Nevertheless here everything becomes more difficult be-

cause of the spiritual apathy of my countrymen who once again let
their educational deficiencies interfere, which becomes more serious
with time.]

Cardoso, however, fought the odds—financial and social—and in the
end, enjoyed the rewards of his hard work. *Eviction on the Street of the
Blacks*, staged in August 1995, highlights the trauma experienced by
black residents of urban tenements known as the Barrio Reus al Sur
when they are forcibly removed from their homes under military or-
ders in 1976. The stated reason was unsafe buildings but the subtext,
as interpreted by Afro-Uruguayans, was the dissolution of black cultural traditions by the military rulers.

The seeds for Cardoso's dramatic interpretation of the barrio had
already been planted in an earlier poem entitled "Negrito del Barrio
Sur"/"Little Black Boy of Barrio Sur," in which the poetic voice con-
trasts mythic, paradaisal Africa with the harsh conditions under
which blacks survive in Uruguay. The speaker proclaims:

> Mas naciste en tierras blancas
> —nieto de esclavos—y tú,
> no habrás de ser otra cosa
> que un niño del Barrio Sur,
> ya marcado por el mito
> de los negros sin virtud.
>
> Sembrarás la desconfianza
> por tu color; y en algún
> desfile oirás los aplausos
> de la falsa multitud
> que se embriaga en los candombes
> de los negros como tú[19]

> [But you were born in white territory
> —grandson of slaves—and you
> wouldn't be anything other
> than a child of Barrio Sur,
> already tainted by the myth
> of blacks without virtue.
>
> You will sow distrust
> with your color; and in some
> parade you will hear the applause
> of the false multitude
> that is inebriated with the candombes
> of blacks like you.]

From birth, the Afro-Uruguayan is condemned, in the larger society's perception, to inferiority without the opportunity to overcome. This is due primarily to history, color, and stereotypes that have evolved, marking blacks as superficial song and dance people. Such an attitude does not allow for an alternate interpretation of the black experience.

This feeling of being dispossessed, without an ancestral home, is a phenomenon that haunts blacks throughout the diaspora. Exile and alienation, combined with overt acts of repression and presented to the public in an intelligible manner account, in part, for the success of *Eviction on the Street of the Blacks*.

Eviction on the Street of the Blacks is a brief, intense work divided into two parts. Its message is conveyed through animated dialogue, music, and the irrepressible drum. There are the appropriate external structural elements—exposition, complication, climax, resolution—that are given internal coherence through images and symbols grounded in the Afro-Uruguayan experience. In discussing "intertextual relations and decodification" in theater and drama, Keir Elam, the eminent drama theoretician, states:

> Appropriate decodificaton of a given text derives above all from the spectator's familiarity with *other* texts (and thus with learned textual rules). By the same token, the genesis of the performance itself is necessarily intertextual: it cannot but bear the traces of other performances at every level, whether that of the written text (bearing generic, structural and linguistic relations with other plays), the scenery (which will "quote" its pictorial or proxemic influences), the actor (whose performance refers back, for the cognoscenti, to other displays), directorial style and so on.[20]

Eviction on the Street of the Blacks represents the epitome of intertextuality. Many of the actors and spectators were performing and re-creating a play amid the very ruins where many of them lived before they were evicted. The decodification of this artistic experience takes place within the larger framework of Afro-Uruguayan existence which is a "living" rather than a "written" text, with the tenement as its central metaphor. The scenery which definitely "quotes" *Eviction on the Street of the Blacks'* "pictorial or proxemic influences," is the Barrio Reus al Sur, the cultural matrix of both participants and spectators/readers.

The theatrical representation of *Eviction on the Street of the Blacks* was received enthusiastically by the public and mainstream critics alike. The play was staged, ironically, amongst the same buildings from which the residents were evicted—under the guise of urban renewal. In a review of the representation, Lauro Marauda, a critic for *La República*, one of Uruguay's most important newspapers, writes:

> en un escenario montado sobre las ruinas de lo que fue el conventillo de Ansina, en San Salvador y Minas, se desarrolla esta pieza que recobra los últimos días anteriores al lanzamiento a la calle de decenas de familias negras, hace ya dieciséis pirulos. Un decreto de la dictadura dejó sin techo a ancianos, mujeres y niños que pasaron a sobrevivir en galpones, peor que los Hereford de la Exposición Rural del Prado, porque éstos reproducen el latifundio y la ganancia de los cabañeros y aquellos no.[21]

> [on a stage constructed upon the ruins of what was the tenement of Ansina at San Salvador and Minas, this drama unfolded, which captures the last days before dozens of black families were thrown into the streets, almost sixteen years ago. A decree by the dictatorship left without a roof old people, women and children who were left to survive in the stockyards worse than the Hereford of the Rural Exposition of Prado Park, because the latter reproduce the land and wealth of the herdsmen and the former no.]

This internal dispersion of the residents of Barrio Reus al Sur was a racist act that had a devastating impact upon Afro-Uruguayans and their sense of community. The temporary relocation to the grounds of the abandoned Martínez Reina textile plant became permanent to the degree that until this day, some of the people evicted still remain without adequate housing.

The primary reason why *Eviction on the Street of the Blacks* received such a positive reaction from a broad Uruguayan societal spectrum is because it touched a national nerve, foregrounding the black experience while interpreting the impact of dictatorship upon everyday people. The play is divided into two acts, with animated dialogue in popular and official registers. The primary setting is the home of Doña Coca, around whom most of the action revolves. The action begins innocently enough with a conversation between Doña Coca and Koulikoro, her nephew, about why he shouldn't marry Ebolova, and other facts of life, and ends with the exodus from the tenement. From the beginning of the play, Doña Coca and Fausto, her husband, are aware that their removal is imminent. The significance of *home* to them is revealed in the following scene:

Fausto.   (Se para) Vení, Coca. Vení y mirá esta calle. Gran parte
             del alma de este pueblo se formó en ella y hoy nadie lo
             toma en cuenta. Seguro, que estos bárbaros, nos echan
             mañana y tiran todo abajo.

Doña Coca.   Lo mismo quieren hacer con el Medio Mundo . . . ¿Y
             adónde va a ir a vivir la gente?

Fausto.   Al corralón donde tanto tiempo durmieron las bestias.
             ¿Total qué somos para ellos más que unos negros can-
             domberos que tomamos vino y los divertimos en car-
             naval? ¿Te das cuenta, ahora, por qué soy tan estricto con
             el muchacho? El va a ser Profesor de Literatura así yo
             tenga que deslomarme trabajando.[22]

[Fausto.   (Stops) Come here, Coca. Come and look at this street. A
             large part of the soul of this community was formed in it
             and today nobody remembers. Surely, those barbarians
             will throw us out tomorrow and tear everything down.

Doña Coca.   They want to do the same with Medio Mundo . . . And
             where will the people go to live?

Fausto.   To the corral where the beasts slept for so long. What are
             we to them other than some black "candomberos" who
             drink wine and entertain them during Carnival? Do you
             understand, now, why I am so strict with the boy? He is
             going to be a Professor of Literature even if I have to work
             myself to death.]

There is not much time for remorse as a colonel arrives and reads
the eviction order, which prompts a predictable response. A request
to delay the move is denied and arguments by the residents are rejected. Anselmo, a neighbor, reasons:

Pero, Coronel, mire que muchos de nosotros somos albañiles y estas
casas están muy bien construidos. No se van a caer así nomás. Coronel, aquí nació mucho de la alegría montevideana. Esta fue una de
las cunas más ilustres del Candombe. Si Ud. hablara con sus com-
pañeros de esa Comisión estoy seguro que nos ayudaría mucho. (9)

[But Colonel, you can see that many of us are builders and these
houses are very well constructed. They are not going to fall down that
way again. Colonel, here much of the happiness of Montevideo was
born. This was one of the most outstanding birthplaces of the Candombe. If you were to speak with your colleagues of the Commission
I'm sure they would help us a lot.]

Anselmo's plea is to no avail. What the colonel views as old buildings is a cultural matrix where Afro-Uruguayan culture is defined and distilled. Faced with the unknown, the black residents seek solace in ritual behavior associated with song and the drum culture:

Solista.   Pobre de mí que en el dolor
             siempre he tenido que vivir,
             fui destinada para parir
             pueblos caídos en el horror.
             Tuve una tierra colossal . . .
             Vino el pirata y me la usurpó.
             Llevó su oro y su caudal,
             después también a mí me llevó.
Coro.   Toca tu tambor
             porque eso alivia el corazón (bis)
Solista: ¡Tamboril!
             Deja de ser mercancía
             vuelve a tu solio de guía
             del alma de nuestra raza
             que se ha quedado sin casa
             sin Protector y sin patria,
             desde que Artigas partió.
                                    (10–11)

[Soloist.   Poor me who in pain
             have always had to live
             I was destined to birth,
             people fallen in horror.
             I had a colossal land . . .
             the pirate came and took it away,
             carried away its gold and riches,
             afterwards he also took me away.
Chorus.   Play your drum
             because that lightens the heart
Soloist.   Drum!
             Stop being merchandise
             return to your throne as guide
             of the soul of our race
             which has remained homeless
             without a Protector and without a homeland
             since Artigas left.]

Afro-Uruguayans are suffering a double sense of exile: first, from the historical external reality of Africa and, second, from the internal de-

nial of their Uruguayan birthright, which dates to the nineteenth
century exile of Artigas. As a subplot, the love affair between
Koulikoro and Ebolova also evolves into a search for roots in mythic
Africa. Her name carries a symbolism that heretofore has escaped
Ebolova. Koulikoro explains:

> Y encontré que Ebolova es una alegre ciudad de Camerún. Como
> aquella bisabuela tuya tenía el mismo nombre es lógico pensar que
> tus antepasados vinieron de allí . . . algo cerca tal vez del Africa Cen-
> tral . . . un hermoso lugar de grandes ríos y fértiles sabanas . . . No te
> gustaría estar allí, y conmigo . . . así abrazados . . . ¿este momento?
> (12)

> [And I found out that Ebolova is a pleasant city in Cameroon. Since
> that great-grandmother of yours had the same name it is logical to
> think that your ancestors came from there . . . somwhere perhaps
> near Central Africa . . . a beautiful place of great rivers and fertile
> plains . . . Wouldn't you like to be there, and with me . . . embraced
> like this . . . this minute?]

Koulikoro's look into an imagined past has provided him, at least on
a superficial level, with the impetus to confront realistically the problem with eviction they are facing. His reaction to Doña Coca's lament,
"Sí este ha sido mi mundo y no puedo abandonarlo de pronto y decir
que me da lo mismo" ["Yes, this has been my world and I cannot
abandon it suddenly and say that it's all the same to me,"] is:

> Tiene razón. ¿Pero qué vamos a hacer si nos echan? Somos la maldita
> raza de Canaán viviendo entre arios: Presidente ario, Ministros arios,
> Generales arios . . . Y desgraciadamente, a Artigas no lo podemos re-
> sucitar. ¡Animo, Doña Coca! ¿Dónde está su estoicismo sudanés? ¿O
> Ud. se sigue sintiendo oriental? Voy a empezar con esta cama . . .
> (comienza a bajar los muebles). (15)

> [You are right. But what are we going to do if they throw us out? We
> are the cursed race of Canaan living amongst Aryans: Aryan Presi-
> dent, Aryan Ministers, Aryan Generals . . . And unfortunately, we can-
> not resuscitate Artigas. Cheer up, Doña Coca! Where is your
> Sudanese stoicism? Or are you still an Uruguayan? I am going to
> begin with this bed . . . (he begins to carry down the furniture].

The theme of blacks as exiles, condemned to wander according to
the biblical myth of Ham, is related symbolically to Afro-Uruguayan

social reality. Their sense of nation has been destroyed as they are unable to transcend Otherness within the society. The Artigas myth is a sustaining one but of no social value under the circumstances. Doña Coca, therefore, has no answer to Koulikoro's query regarding her Uruguayan identity, since their African origins have been constructed on the basis of *myth,* in the true sense of the word.

Toward the end of his review of *Eviction on the Street of the Blacks,* Lauro Marauda observes:

> los negros demuestran en esta obra que pueden hacer algo más que de domésticas, porteros, y cantar como la cigarra al son de las lonjas. Hay que ver si los blancos somos capaces de poner un granito de arena a la dignidad, al buen arte y al peor bache que tiene nuestra ciudad: el del prejuicio de una falsa y estúpida superioridad racial. Y ojo, que de arios y de locos, varios tienen bastante. (3)

> [Blacks demonstrate in this work that they can be more than domestics, doormen and sing like the cicada to the tune of drums. We have to see if we white people are capable of lending a grain of salt to dignity, to good art, and to the worst attitude our city has: that of the prejudice of a false and stupid racial superiority. And look out, of Aryans and crazies there are enough.]

This play seems to have been instructive, at least among some of the more enlightened members of Uruguayan society. This is the most important drama published by an Afro-Uruguayan writer and can be read in a number of symbolic and literal levels. *Eviction on the Street of the Blacks* is the dramatic representation of the fears of Afro-Uruguayans as well as their hopes for a better day.

In postcolonial literatures, Ashcroft and his coeditors inform us, "the construction or demolition of houses or buildings in post-colonial locations is a recurring and evocative figure for the problematic of post-colonial identity in works from very different societies."[23] Throughout Afro-Uruguayan literature a sense of loss—of culture, of a sense of belonging, for permanency—permeates the discourse. In Cardoso's play, we are no longer concerned only with the destruction of the physical environment, the flora and the fauna, or the elimination of traditional sites of resistance by black maroons, such as hills, forests, and swamps. Rather, *Eviction on the Street of the Blacks* dramatizes an attack upon a type of cultural maroonage, a syncretization of African remnants and New World values, which has sustained black people throughout the diaspora. Herein resides its power as a work of art.

Cardoso has also written several other dramas, one *entitled El Medio Mundo de Juan/Juan's Medio Mundo,* which also deals with the tenement culture and which he is seeking resources to stage, including actors (blacks, almost entirely). Cardoso's most recent plays are titled *Los Condenados / The Condemned* and *Esclava y Ama / Slave and Mistress* as he continues to be productive on the Uruguayan theatrical scene.

Given his most recent *negrista* antecedents, the Teatro Negro Independiente in particular, the significance of Cardoso's works cannot be overstated. He has also foregrounded serious aspects of Afro-Uruguayan existence, such as the permanent sense of exile and adherence to the ancestral drum culture. Cardoso presents a positive image of black culture in Uruguay while at the same time reminding us that from the perspective of "Candombe," the brief interlude by Roberto Cisnero in 1942 to the appearance of *Eviction on the Street of the Blacks* more half than a century later, not much has changed regarding color, class, and the "place" of blacks in that country.

In his poetry, prose, and drama, Jorge Emilio Cardoso articulates the fundamental postcolonial theme of exile and the attendant concern with place and displacement. These attitudes underscore the conceptual basis of Cardoso's drama as well as the plays of Afro-Uruguayan writers from José Isabelino Gares to the present. The black Other remains from a drama perspective, unfortunately, at the margins seeking redress from the center, to no avail.

6

Richard Piñeyro:
The Afro-Uruguayan Writer as Invisible Man

WHEN ANALYZING A LITERARY TRADITION SUCH AS THE AFRO-Uruguayan, one has to be careful not to categorize or stereotype based upon preconceived notions. Over the years, many voices have emerged that must be dealt with for their intrinsic merit as well as their extrinsic value. The fact that Piñeyro does not dwell upon his blackness does not lessen the degree of suffering communicated to the reader. Somehow, the message is conveyed that this disaffection is caused by his social and ethnic situations, as well as his self-perception. While Richard Piñeyro seldom addresses overtly his position as a black Uruguayan subject, the amount of pain, suffering, and anguish activated by the poetic voice is not totally divorced from the poet's ethnic background and his poverty. Afro-Uruguayans who rejected the official version of ethnic relations in that country have, since the beginnings of their ability to interpret their own circumstance and present their concerns as marginalized individuals, created a counterdiscourse expressing their dissatisfaction with the status quo. This is evident from the nineteenth century to the present, even in some of the less vociferous writers.

In spite of the historical trajectory of Afro-Uruguayans as society's "others," many have been reluctant to accept the reality present since slavery that there is discrimination and racism based upon skin color in that country. Yet blacks in Uruguay are quick to point out that even as slaves they worked on ranches and in the domestic sphere, which made them closer to their more "humane" owners than slaves in Cuba or the United States, for instance, who allegedly suffered more. There is apparently a built-in psychological denial as a defense mechanism that allows many Afro-Uruguayans to accept the lie that they are equal to whites as guaranteed by the Constitution. Miscegenation and acculturation, supposedly, helped to make it so.

While the majority of socially aware black writers in Uruguay are quick to proclaim their ethnic identity, this is not true for the late Richard Piñeyro. Until he was featured in a recent issue of *El País Cultural*, very little was known about this talented poet who was born in 1956 and committed suicide in 1998. He had been profiled, briefly, in Alberto Britos's third anthology of black Uruguayan poets (see pages 91-93). Piñeyro published three books of poetry: *Quiero tener una muchacha que se llame Beba/I Want to Have a Girl Named Beba* (1983), *Cartas a la vida/Letters to Life* (1985), and *El otoño y mis cosas/ Autumn and My Things* (1992). *Palabra antigua/Ancient Word* (1999) was published posthumously. He left, also unpublished, "Poemas dentro de ella" and "Todo se vuelve jazmín," a novel manuscript.

In his brief introductory essay in *El País Cultural*, "Recuerdo de Richard Piñeyro: una poesía esencial"/ "Memory of Richard Piñeyro: An Essential Poetry," Luis Bravo provides some biographical details regarding Piñeyro:

> Fue un poeta íntimo y apasionado, de un lirismo afincado en lo cotidiano y algo alejado de los postulados estéticos de su generación. Había nacido en 1956 en Montevideo, y tenía apenas diecisiete años cuando cayó preso de la dictadura militar. Los maltratos recibidos en el Penal de Libertad donde permaneció hasta 1980, debilitaron su salud física y mental, pero no consiguieron apagar su inteligencia y su capacidad creadora.[1]

> [He was an intimate and passionate poet rooted in daily life and somewhat distanced from the aesthetic directions of his generation. He was born in 1956 in Montevideo and was barely seventeen years old when he was imprisoned by the military dictatorship. The harsh treatment he received in the Penal de Libertad prison where he remained until 1980, weakened his physical and mental health, but did not succeed in snuffing out his intelligence and creative capacity.]

Although the impact of the Uruguayan dictatorship upon the Afro-Uruguayan community has been dramatized profoundly by Jorge Emilio Cardoso in *El desalojo de la calle de los negros/ Eviction on the Street of the Blacks* Piñeyro is the first black writer that we know of who suffered its impact firsthand. At the time of his imprisonment, Richard Piñeyro was characterized by those who knew him as dissident, but certainly a seventeen-year-old boy in his circumstances did not represent a serious threat to the military dictatorship. According to Luis Bravo, Piñeyro's career as a poet actually began during his imprisonment (1973–1980) where "Prosa, poesía y algo más"/"Prose, Poetry and Something More," his manuscript, was first circulated in 1974. The importance of this precursor manuscript is that one of the poems included, "El día de la noche"/"The Day of Night," is Piñeyro's only text that refers directly to his blackness:

> Esta piel negra
> que me cubre los sueños
> esta piel
> anochecida por la rueda de la historia
> este remolino de noche
> que viene desde siglos reclamando
> un aire de justicia a la mañana
> será de todos los colores
> el horizonte anhelado de mi raza.[2]

> [This black skin
> which covers my dreams
> this skin
> blackened by the wheel of history
> this whirlpool of night
> which comes from centuries after demanding
> an air of justice from the morning
> shall be of all colors
> the longed for horizon of my race.]

The title, "The Day of Night" embodies an implicit dialectic of tension between the negative historical perception of blackness alongside the positive future need to overcome the negativity attached to this color. It is a poem about equality, of lifting the stigma attached to blackness in hope for a better day. The fight is not new; rather, in the perception of the speaker, it has reached a crescendo in the quest to eliminate stereotypes and provide equality for all. Anaphora (*esta/este*), as well as the dialectical opposition of the night/dawn metaphor, stresses the tension of the present situation and the need to change.

I Want to Have a Girl Named Beba is Piñeyro's first published book of poetry. This title comes from a verse, "y tener una muchacha que se llame Beba"/ "to have a girl named Beba," by Julio Huasi, the Argentine writer. Regarding Piñeyro's book, Luis Bravo writes, "En lo temático aparece, obsesiva, la dialéctica de la luz y lo sombrío. Este rasgo remite tanto a lo social como a una más universal condición existencial" ["In the thematics, the dialectic between light and shadow seem obsessive. This trait addresses the social as well as the universal existential condition"].

I Want to Have a Girl Named Beba consists of twenty poems in free verse with a plethora of thematic concerns. It is poetry of alienation, replete with memories of family and friends, of life and death, of love and loss. The motif of Communion during the ritualistic sharing of food and wine recurs throughout the volume. Poem number III—"A Emilio"/"To Emilio"—is indicative of this tendency:

> Usted y yo, compadre
> sentados alrededor de un vaso de vino.
> Usted y yo
> compadre
> para que su silencio
> se abrace a mi silencio,
> para que usted me diga
> para que yo le diga
> para que nos digamos
> si la Ñata queda embarazada
> si el alquiler quinientos pesos
> si Mauré o Goyeneche no me joda
> si fue gol o la sacaron en la línea
> si el domingo tendrá olores de buseca
> si podar los transparentes significa
> pegarle una trompada por la espalda a noviembre.
>
> Usted y yo, compadre
> sentados alrededor de un vaso de vino.
> Usted y yo, compadre
> atiendamé
> y así es la vida.[3]
>
> [You and I, partner
> seated around a glass of wine
> you and I
> partner
> so that your silence
> embraces my silence
> so that you tell me
> so that I tell you
> so that we tell each other

if Ñata is pregnant
if loaning five hundred pesos
if Mauré or Goyeneche doesn't screw me
if it were a goal or offside
if Sunday will have pleasant smells
if pruning the transparent
punching November in the back.

You and I, partner
seated around a glass of wine.
You and I, partner
listen up
and that's life.]

Poem III, as are many of the selections in this volume, is structured around an apostrophe, an interior monologue devoted to a significant past event. In this instance, the poetic voice is trying to engage in a dialog with his "compadre" in an effort to discover what is transpiring in the world that they once shared. Sharing a glass of wine is the triggering event for the conjecture regarding everyday topics of conversation prefaced by "if." Anaphora is the predominant rhetorical device which reiterates the friendship bonds that begin and end the poem with "you and I, partner." The theme is communication on a human level.

The shared experience of individuals of common origins within a community is also the concern in Poem IV:

Tu dolor
mi dolor
el de Pedro.
Nosotros los de la caricia ebria
los del cielo negado que no sabe de estrellas
los que pretendemos repartir el sol como una hostia
nosotros los que tenemos un payaso acunado en tango
                    por corazón.

Nosotros
hijos de una margarita prostituta que creció en el baldío
hijos de algún cardo pendenciero
nosotros
pájaros de barrio que gorjeamos de hambre
murguistas nocturnos que salimos a romperle los candados
                    al viento.
Nosotros los de la primavera remendada

nosotros
inquilinos del dolor que laten en la espera.

(8)

[Your pain
my pain
that of Pedro.
Those of us of the drunken caress
those of the heaven denied that knows nothing of stars
those with whom we pretend to share the sun like a host
those of us who have a clown engaged in tango
                    for a heart.

We
children of a daisy prostitute which grew in a wasteland
children of a troublesome thistle
We
neighborhood birds who warbled from hunger
we nocturnal actors who went out to break the locks
                    of the wind.

We of the mended spring
We
tenants of pain who lie in wait.]

Collective suffering is the point of departure (your/mine/his) as
again through interior monologue the apostrophic poetic voice attempts to discover common ground in origins. What is encountered
though, is negativity as those of uncertain origins suffer an adverse
societal and cosmic fate. Those of the "drunken caress" in the first
stanza eventually become children of a "daisy prostitute," a "worri-
some thistle," "birds of the barrio who warbled with hunger." Here
the poetic voice uses nonhuman metaphors to exacerbate the condition of those who are perceived as folkloric as exemplified through
the allusions to the "tango" and the "murga," popular art forms. In
the final analysis, they remain as the incarnation of pain hoping for
a better life. The entire poem is a metaphor for existence as the
speaker views the situation from the perspectives of alienation and
rejection.

Poem V, "Carta al negro"/"Letter to the Black Man," is one of the
more optimistic selections in the book, to the extent that it remembers good times and projects them into the future. The poetic voice
measures the passage of time in relation to the seasons as it tries to
project what is transpiring, from a distance, with family and friends.

There is nostalgia for the simple things in life, as human existence and natural cyclicality are inextricably bound in life's trajectory.

"Letter to the Black Man" ends on a series of rhetorical questions:

> Qué más puedo decirte
> que estaremos todos juntos algún día
> que Estela va a preparar los tallarines
> que Alicia bailará con su lucero
> que pondremos un mantel grande debajo de la higuera
> con la alegría sentada a nuestra mesa
> y el sol brindará con nuestras risas
> y el cielo
> (tan macanudo)
> se pondrá el mejor de sus celestes,
> y le pediremos más cubiertos al vecino
> y al vino le llamaremos Ramón
> y guirnaldas en el patio
> y yo qué sé, negro
> tanta
> tanta borrachera de alegría.
> Bueno, te voy dejando.
> Saludos de toda la familia
> la Ñata, Juan, José, Pepe
> las madreselvas
> los transparentes.
>
> Chau
>
> (10)

> [What more can I say to you
> that we will be together some day
> that Estela is going to prepare the pasta
> that Alicia will dance with a star
> that we will put a large tablecloth under the fig tree
> with joy seated around our table
> and the sun will salute our smiles
> and the sky
> (so fantastic)
> will put on its best displays,
> and we will ask the neighbor for more silverware
> and we will call the wine Ramón
> and garlands in the patio
> and what do I know, "negro"
> so much
> so much drunken happiness.
> Well, I'm gone.

Greetings from the family
Ñata, Juan, José, Pepe
the honeysuckles
the clearings.

Chau]

The poetic voice realizes the impossibility of recapturing the days of happiness, which are now nothing more than a romantic fantasy, it seems. This symbolic projection ends though as reality reasserts itself in the form of an unpleasant present. The epistolary mode is employed in this sad parting of the ways as an accumulation of events that weigh heavily upon his memory are internalized and let go.

This sense of loss, of absence articulated by the speaker, extends to the motif of love as well. The poetic voice recounts a trajectory from childhood to maturity. In Poem VIII, for instance, the relationship is one of innocence until the realities of life finally surface. The evolution is from "I loved her when she went to the store to buy a notebook/and I went running to steal birds (kisses) from her fleshy/lips," to "Later/later came life with its tango of purples and greys" (12).

The greatest sense of estrangement is expressed, however, in Poem XX, which serves to summarize the entire collection:

Saber que estás tan lejos
que las horas pasan
que los días pasan
y no saber una noticia
algo de vos;
ir buscando entre las sombras
entre la niebla de recuerdos
entre el moho de esperanzas viejas
que habitan en mis huesos
un gesto tuyo
(nunca te dije: el otoño fue el orfebre
que talló con sus melancolías aquel gesto)
una palabra tuya
(dijiste: no sé, miro los árboles
seas ramas delgadas que perdieron sus hojas
soy una rama de esas: tu amor: eran mis hojas)

Saber que estás tan lejos
que vendrá el invierno con sus ojos de frío
que arribará la primavera y en su vientre habrá almendras
y no saber

y no saber de vos
una noticia
algo . . .

(30)

[To know that you are so far away
that hours go by
that days go by
and not having any news
something about you
to go searching amongst the shadows
amongst the cloud of reminiscences
amongst the mildew of old wishes
that reside in my bones
your gesture
(I never told you: autumn was the goldsmith
which fashioned with its sadness that gesture)
your word
(you said: I don't know, I look at trees
may they be slim branches which lost their leaves
I am one of those branches: your love: were my leaves)

To know that you are so far away
that winter will come with its cold eyes
that spring will rise up and in its stomach there will be almonds
and not know
and not know about you
some news
something . . .]

The enduring characteristics of love are first juxtaposed to the re-
lentlessness of nature and then coalesced in the regenerative image
of a tree. Metaphors of time and distance amplify the sense of loss,
both physical and emotional, inherent in this selection. The importance of *I Want to Have a Girl Named Beba* in the poetic trajectory of
Richard Piñeyro is that it outlines a number of themes—such as love,
death, alienation, time, identity—that will be treated in depth in subsequent volumes.

In *Letters to Life* (1985), Piñeyro utilizes the epistolary method to
express more of the deep sentiments that surfaced in the previous
volume. *Letters,* however, is totally in prose that maintains the same di-
alogic intensity expressed in Piñeyro's poetry. One of the central concerns of the writer is lost love, which in most instances is a fading
memory from his contemporary position.

There are a number of letters dealing with women and relationships. In the "Carta a Laura"/ "Letter to Laura" the author summarizes why his attitudes may have more to do with fantasy than reality: "My true passion is women. I look them in the eye and try to seduce them, but because I am black and ugly they don't give me the time of day."[4] The only other occasion on which the author refers to himself as black is in "Letter from the Black Man to His Companion": "The man who is not sure of himself doesn't propose social change. He will not soon perceive of himself as a man" (35). This appears to be an attempt to have the "compañero" define himself as a socially committed human being.

The majority of the letters of substance are devoted to love and women, as evidenced in two selections entitled "Carta a ella"/ "Letter to Her" and "Carta a mi primer amor"/ "Letter to My First Love" in addition to the aforementioned "Letter to Laura." These texts reveal Piñeyro as a romantic poet who is sensitive and passionate. "Letter to Her" is illustrative of these tendencies:

A veces cuando miro por la pequeña ventana que tengo, pienso en tí. Es hermoso morirse con el crepúsculo junto a tu imagen. Fluyo como un río, bajo los cielos violetas, azules y rojos, entre pastos, espigas y pájaros. Tu imagen es un beso de rocío a mis labios de tierra. Y pienso en tí. Recuerdo nuestras tardes de buñuelos y mate. Cuando mi silencio se posaba en las aguas de tu silencio. Y pienso en tí. Recuerdo tu capacidad de encontrar pedacitos de cármica junto a la costa. Y, yo mediocre, pobrecito, queriendo recoger caracoles de tu mirada. Nunca te dije. Amarte es estar junto a mi mismo. Es estar en la casa de tu pecho, solo, rodeado de buñuelos, mate y silencio. (17)

[At times when I look through the small window I have, I think about you. It is beautiful to die at dusk next to your image. I flow like a river under violet, blue, and red skies, amongst grass, wheat, and birds. Your image is a kiss of dew on my earthly lips. And I think about you. I remember our evenings of sweets and maté. When my silence rested in the waters of your silence. And I think about you. I remember your ability to find pieces of seashell near the coast. And I mediocre, poor thing, wishing to gather shells from your gaze. I never told you. To love you is to be next to myself. It is being in the sanctuary of your chest, surrounded by sweets, maté and silence.]

From the subject position of isolation the woman is gazed upon through a prism imbued with natural imagery that fuses with the poetic voice's sense of being. Thoughts and memories serve to reconstruct a bygone era of romantic meandering as the speaker uses nature to locate the object of his desires. "I am not worthy" is the attitude of anxiety expressed although he is seeking a union of body and spirit that will last forever.

The second "Letter to Her" recounts a missed opportunity to have a woman who chose Alvaro, a fellow prisoner, as a companion instead of the speaker. The unmistakeable tone of jealousy and envy surfaces as he refers to Alvaro as "somebody who life chose by chance, not by merit, to put him before your gaze, before your desires and uncertainties" (26). This sense of inadequacy results in self pity and a questioning of the speaker's sense of self. Since Alvaro's ethnic background is not mentioned, the reader is not aware of whether color was a factor in this triangle.

The need to communicate, so prevalent throughout Piñeyro's poetry, is the prevailing motif of the "Letter to My First Love." The reconstruction of past events through memory sets the tone of the letter: "I don't know if you remember; I opened the door the other day and was greeted by a smell, a breath of honeysuckles and geraniums" (30). The sensory perception of flowers triggers the memory of intimate times spent with his first love, which is a precious recollection inspired by the forces of nature. He remembers her moonlike smile and compares her to geraniums that have grown in the wasteland of their social reality. In spite of the obstacles: "tus diecisiete años decididos a elegirme, a mí, un pobrecito, a elegirme en medio de plazas y banderas, para ganarme la sangre, para buscarme los todavías de la piel, el inicio de la barba" ["your seventeen years decided to choose me, a poor thing, to choose me in the midst of plazas and flags, to earn blood, to find in me the to-be's of the skin, the beginning of the beard"]. It is she who facilitates the transition for him from adolescence to manhood.

Their destiny is linked to that of the seasons of nature. Spring has now been transformed to winter and the ensuing toll upon their relationship is evident as the initial positive images clash with the reality of the present situation: "I lost my tin huts and my wine, and did not find , my love, the transparencies of my barrio street, I remained anchored in the port of sadness" (31). Final references in the letter are to death, desolation, and suicide.

Most of the letters in this collection, at one level or the other, question the nature of human existence. "Sad Letter" poses fundamental questions but offer no answers:

¿Qué es el hombre de nuestra época? Un amor que no se dio, suela
gastadas, un poco de alcohol que navega pecho adentro, el recuerdo
de haber visto alguna vez el ferrocarril, una rabia loca de pájaro que
no quiere morir; y siempre, siempre, la honda tristeza en los ojos de
estar vivo.(21)

[What is the man of our times? A love affair gone bad, worn out
shoes, a taste of alcohol which flows within the chest, the memory of
having seen the railroad once, the crazy rage of a bird which does
not want to die; and always, always, the deep sadness of being alive in
the eyes.]

This existential focus, initiated in Piñeyro's first volume of poems, is
fundamental to his brief excursion into the epistolary genre.

Autumn and My Things (1992) is another step in Piñeyro's questioning of the nature of human existence. His preoccupation with
love, time, and destiny is prevalent throughout the volume as well as
allusions to the private life of the poet. This latter tendency is evident
in "Confession of R.P.":

> Todo fue muy triste
> triste aquellos trapos violetas
> que yo guardaba escondidos
> y descubrir un día
> que me habían hecho un traje para el
> /registro civil.
>
> Y yo entiendo: la sociedad está mal,
> pero fue muy triste
> yo, pirata, salir a ver a mi muchacha
> y volver muchos años después
> con los riñones destrozados por las
> /patadas
>
> y el barquito con las velas rotas
> por haber atracado
> en silencios e inviernos.[5]
>
> [Everything was very sad
> and those violet rags
> which I kept hidden
> and to find out one day
> that they had made me an outfit for the
> /registry office

And I understand: society is bad
but it was very sad
me, a pirate, going out to see my girl
and returning many years later
with my kidneys destroyed by
            /kicks

and the little ship with its broken sails
for having docked
in silences and winters.

Images of sadness and neglect dominate the initial stanzas of the poem as the poetic "I" reminisces about past incidents that have structured his life. His current situation is blamed upon an evil society of which he is victim and that is responsible for his personal failure. Youthful innocence is transformed into mature cynicism, which questions the lack of freedom and individuality. This is evident in the pirate and seafaring metaphors around which the last two stanzas are built. The underlying contradiction is that individuals are only as free as society allows them to be.

More importantly, "Confesson of R.P." answers the question, perhaps, regarding why Piñeyro was imprisoned. The speaker informs us: "Me, a pirate, going out to see my girl/ and returning many years later/ with my kidneys destroyed by /kicks." He perceives himself as an innocent victim of an unjust society.

The majority of poems in *Autumn and My Things* are of an introspective nature as the poet is in a constant dialogue with himself regarding existence and destiny. The untitled poem dedicated "To Mirito" initiates a trend prevalent throughout:

Miro la oscuridad
mi humilde mundo
mi soledad
mi cansada esperanza.

El tiempo fue tiempo y rama.
El tejido laborioso de los hombres, gente,
            /necesarios días.

Quizás haya una mañana.
El día no pregunta, ni se justifica:
            el sol sale: es.

Habría mucho para decir
mundos para callar.

El silencio es trabajo, fin;
Dios creó cuando calló, ahí, entonces.
Hubo raíces, brío: primavera.
Hubo ramas, las mías,
la savia necesaria que durará lo necesario.
Tiempo, tiempo y cielo e infinito cielo.
Y en él ramas, mis ramas que perecen,
                    /ramas que perecen.
Penar infinitesimal, dolor infinitesimal,
                    /calma, sosiego: nada.

(11)

[I look at the darkness
my humble world
my solitude
my tired hope.

Time was time and branch
The laborious weaving of men, people
                    /necessary days
Perhaps there is a tomorrow.
The day does not ask, nor justifies itself:
                    the sun rises: it is.
There would be a lot to say
worlds to silence.
Silence is work, end;
God created when he shut up, there, then.
There were roots, spirit: spring.
There were branches, mine
the necessary sap which would last sufficiently.
Time, time and heaven and infinite sky.
And in its branches, my branches that die
                    /branches that die.
Infinitesimal suffering, infinitesimal pain,
                    /calm, peace: nothing.]

This poem espoused a worldview of alienation and self-pity, of an individual caught up in the indifferent cycles of nature. Time is the theme of the poem; the past has determined what is transpiring in the present without any assurance of a future. Meanwhile the individual suffers immeasurably, and dies like a mere tree branch, a metaphor for a component of the human race. Within the poet's deterministic worldview, however, all hope is not lost.

One of the positive images the poetic voice preserves is that of the mother figure—strong, devoted, enduring, and unfulfilled. The following poem exemplifies this feeling as she performs her daily chores:

> La ropa tendida al sol.
>
> el esfuerzo de mamá
>   sus rayos X
>   su gordura
>
>   usual
>   acostumbrada.
>
> El rostro de mamá
> cansado de otros rostros
> cansado de plantas regadas
>
>   de cosas que quiso
>   de cosas que no pudo
>   con quejas
>   sin quejas.
>   (40)
>
> [Clothing hung out in the sun
>
> the strength of mama
>   her X-rays
>   her fatness
>
>   normal
>   expected
>
> The face of mama
> tired of the other faces
> tired of watering plants
>
>   of things she wanted
>   of things she could not have
>   with complaints
>   without complaints.

The image of a sacrificing, self-denying mother who dies without realizing her dreams pervades this poem. The strength of the mother is juxtaposed to the tiredness of a life of labor without rewards. "Complaining without complaining" attests to the dialectic nature of the mother's existence, as she silently shoulders the many burdens confronting her:

> El sol
> mamá: y la vida de mamá

> sus manos
> su ropa tendida
> el cuadro en la cómoda de sus veinte años
> los sueños que compartió
> sus sueños que vagabundearon
> hasta llegar y alcanzar el silencio
> destino de los sueños, de mamá, y de los
>   /sueños, silencios
>   graves, densos,
>   silencios de mamá.
>
> (40)

> [The sun
> mama: and the life of mama
>   her hands
>   her clothing hung out
> the painting in the twenty-year-old chest of drawers
> the dreams she shared
> her dreams that roamed
> until arriving and reaching silence
> destiny of the dreams, of mama, and of the
>   /dreams, grave
>   silences, dense
>   silences of mama.]

Her unarticulated dreams are never realized as both life and aspirations are shrouded in silence. The sun is placed in ironic juxtaposition to the poetic object and serves as a reminder of the instability of her life and the passage of time:

> La ropa tendida.
> El sol que sale, promete y luego sale.
> Las palabras repetidas.
> Las veces que me quejé
>   o callé.
>
> Destino de los sueños, míos, y de los
>   /sueños: silencios
>   graves, densos, rostros y otros
>   /rostros cansados.
>
>   Un poco de gordura.
>   Unos rayos X.
>   Sueños, y sus destinos, el
>   /silencio, sol

que sale o se va
sale o se va.

y otros rostros
y otras cuerdas
de ropa
y otros silencios.

Mamá.
Hijos.
Cariños.

(41)

[The clothing hung out.
The sun which appears, promises and then leaves.
The repeated words.
The times I complained
or shut up.

Destiny of dreams, mine, and of the
/dreams: silences
serious, dense, faces and other
/tired faces.
a little fatness
Some X-rays
Dreams, and their destiny, the
/silence, sun

which comes out or goes away
comes out or goes away.

and other faces
and other pieces
of clothing
and other silences.

Momma.
Children.
Love.]

The indeterminate nature of her existence is underscored through the deft use of anaphora and alliteration. Ultimately, the weight of time and lifestyle simply wears the mother down. Health—overweight (fatness) and medicine (X-rays) are factors involved in her demise. The poetic voice is left with only memories of this life of sacrifice and abnegation.

Throughout *Autumn and My Things,* Piñeyro questions the meaning of human existence. There is a constant examining of his "place" in the universe:

> ¿Qué es la vida?
> qué engaño cruel
> qué sueño portentoso, magnificiente,
>   /todopoderoso
>
> que busca, busca y busca
>   para encontrar
>   un fósforo
>   un boleto
>   una rama sola y sin misterio:
>   /rama triste.
>   (56)

> [What is life?
> what cruel deceit
> what marvellous, magnificent, dream,
>   /all powerful
>
> that searches, searches and searches
>   in order to find
>   a match
>   a ticket
>   a lonely branch without mystery:
>   /sad branch.]

The poetic devices of polysyndeton and anaphora are used effectively to convey the sense of ironic uncertainty implied in the rhetorical nature of the question posed. "What," "a," "without" trivializes and exacerbates the situation of humans who in their current state are no more than an inanimate "branch," figuratively and literally, a not too special component of the animal kingdom.

Fundamentally, however, the poetic voice is questioning God, with whom he seeks communion in death:

> El hombre fue
>   vio el rostro de su creador
>   y lo amó, lo amó, lo amó
> hasta quedarse Dios, hombre, creador,
>   rama.
>   (56)

[Man went
        saw the face of his creator
        and loved him, loved him, loved him
    until God became man, creator,
            branch.]

There is a final synthesis of the creator and the created through the power of love.

In the introduction to *Ancient Word* (1999), Carlos Brandy writes: "*Palabra antigua* es un poemario aluvional, donde un hombre estremecido de terror ante el espectáculo del mundo, se defiende con palabras. A veces sobriamente, a veces abundante como el mar que golpea empecinado. A veces cosecha belleza y esperanza, a veces sólo horror y desasosiego"[6] ["*Ancient Word* is an overflowing poetry collection, where a man terrified by the spectacle of the world, defends himself with words. At times calmly, at times forcefully, like the sea which batters stubbornly. At times it harvest beauty and hope, at times only horror and unease"]. In *Ancient Word* alienation becomes even more pronounced than in the preceding volumes. The speaker is constantly acted upon by his circumstances rather than being in control of his own destiny.

Deambulo por mi soledad
llena de rostros queridos muchos
queridos como puede un corazón
ardor, sangre, algo de tibia hipocresía.

Rostros, rostros, que prometo defender.
Los seres que amo, construyo o traiciono
mientras las heridas me envejecen, me vencen
mientras las heridas me hacen más dulce,

más feo, más triste, más feroz para defender
alguna alegría que viene al huerto y el huerto
        pronto olvida.
No soy una linda persona. Me equivoco mucho.
Soy esta pequeñez, más hijos, más lluvias, más
        olvidos.

Los días pasan y hieren; el mundo lastima
        rompe sueños.
Soy poco, tiemblo de flores, desengaños, cielos,
        vanidades.
Soy el mundo y estoy en el mundo. Morirán los
        días,

Me hieren, el mundo lastima, rompe sueños,
mis huesos, la luz, el goce. Seré olvido viejo,
       tonto, tonto, y feo.

Los días fueron y la vida latió efímera y loca.
Mi hija juega con los trapos que el sol da a los
       hombres.
Duele esto. Maravillosa luz que todo tocas y
       mentiras creas.
Un rostro me reclama. Esto pequeño que soy,
       sufre, se oxida.

Este pequeño que soy, esta pobre amargura, que
       se expande, luce, fracasa, y luce.
                      (10–11)

[I wander through my solitude
filled with the faces of dearly beloveds
loved like a heart can with
fervor, blood, a little warm hypocrisy.

Faces, faces, I promise to defend.
The beings I love, construct or betray
while the wounds age me, conquer me
while the wounds make me sweeter,

uglier, sadder, more ferocious to defend
some happines which comes into the garden and the garden
       quickly forgets.
I am not a pretty person. I make many mistakes.
I am this smallness, more children, more
       forgetfulness.

The days go by and wounds; the world harms
       destroys dreams.
I am small, I tremble with flowers, disillusions, skies,
       vanities.
I am the world and I am in the world. The days will
       die,
They hurt me, the world harms, destroys dreams,
my bones, light, pleasure. I will be an old memory,
       stupid, stupid, and ugly.

Days passed and life pulsated ephemeral and crazy.
My daughter plays with the rags the sun gives to
       men.
That hurts. Marvellous light, which touches all and
       creates lies.

A face claims me. This little thing that I am,
    suffers, rusts.

This little thing that I am, this poor bitterness, which
    expands, shines, fails, and shines.]

This separation from self, others, and society is forcefully presented as solitude becomes a metaphor for the speaker's relationship to others. The frustration and impotence felt when faced with a set of insurmountable obstacles are apparent where the "beloved faces" are betrayed by heartfelt hypocrisy in the first stanza. These faces haunt the speaker throughout this poem as self-pity and guilt predominate.

"I am not a pretty person. I make many mistakes". . . / "I am small, I tremble with flowers, disillusions, skies, vanities." The poetic "I" and its confessional mode reveals the deep-seated anguish of the speaker, who is as much to blame for his plight as society. Yet this symbiotic relationship does not change: "I am the world and I am in the world. The days will die,/they hurt me, the world harms, destroys dreams." Caught up in the temporal cycles of an uncaring universe as an "old memory" the speaker's alienated, destitute plight is handed down to the next generation: "My daughter plays with the rags the sun gives to men. That hurts." Self-denigration and suffering are the legacies the speaker will leave, but why? Why is he so bitter, wounded, fractured, dismembered, ambivalent about himself and his society? Could it be related to his position as a black subject? In Piñeyro's worldview, being black is just another condition imposed upon man to make him suffer.

This poem is representative of the entire volume to the extent that the speaker perceives of himself as a victim, as object of society's evil deeds. Consequently the material world is presented as a hostile environment over which he exercises no control, cannot escape from, and is condemned to suffer: "The weight of pain falls upon my shoulders, breasts, hearts . . . I walk wounded. The pain rests in my side" (11). Throughout these collections of poems by Richard Piñeyro, the speaker presents himself as a martyr, a Christlike figure who has been victimized for being who he is.

The passage of time, with the specter of death looming ominously in the background, is prevalent throughout Piñeyro's poetry as well and reaches its culminating point in *Ancient Word.* "Life passes me by" begins the first stanza of one poem. "Years have passed" initiates the second. The speaker then turns to a Latin cliché, "*tempus fugit*" to assess his situation:

Pienso cosas.
La mano acaricia sabia como una mujer que
                    cose
los años idos, los recuerdos que el invierno
                    atesora
con la ternura del árbol que dio sombra, gimió y
                    partió al oscurecer.

El invierno cuenta viejas alegrías de aquel
                    camino ancho
de sauces jóvenes, y un cielo azul donde los
                    gorriones latían
para cantar fervores que los hombres tenaces
                    exigían
al tiempo, a la soledad, a las viejas lágrimas que
                    edificaron edades.

Es cierto que ya pasó el tiempo de la fiebre y la
                    rosa.
                                          (16)

[I think about things.
My hand caresses knowingly like a woman who
                    sews
the years gone by, the memories that winter
                    stores up
with the tenderness of the tree which gave shade, moaned and
                    left at dusk.
Winter counts old joys of that
                    wide road
of young willows, and a blue sky where
                    sparrows pulsated
to sing praises that tenacious men
                    demanded
to time, to solitude, to the old tears which
                    built ages.

It is true that the time of fever and the rose has
                    already passed.]

Remembrances of time past as a motif is framed within the archetypal context of winter as the season of death and dying. Humans
are caught in the uncaring cyclicality of nature. The "wide road" of
life, tempered by time, solitude, and pain terminates, inevitably, in
death.

The winter/death metaphor structures most of the poem; "Winter is painful but it shows wisely the infinitesimal/dying of the leaves" (17). Incredibly, all hope is not lost as the speaker previews an optmistic future, ironically:

> Habrá otros mundos y otros capitanes. Habrá
> otras mañanas,
> y en mi pequeño credo sincero habitará hierba
> verde, grácil, efímera.
>
> (17)

> [There will be other worlds and other captains. There
> will be other tomorrows,
> and in my small sincere creed will reside
> green grass, graceful, ephemeral.]

The ambivalence inherent in the verses of the final stanzas of this poem is reflective of the overall worldview implicit in Piñeyro's poetry regarding questions of existence, life, and death. While there is total discontent with the present, perhaps the future will spawn a positive creative effort as well as a more secure sense of self. For Richard Piñeyro, the poet, neither of these dreams is fulfilled.

Richard Piñeyro presents a different dimension of the Afro-Uruguayan experience. He was a black writer who did not overtly manifest his ethnicity in the majority of his poetry. Nevertheless, Piñeyro's existential anguish and alienation from the society of his time locates him within the ideological currents of contemporary black expression in Uruguay.

In his short life, Richard Piñeyro developed a hermetic, less overtly expressive style of Afro-Uruguayan discourse than that of his counterparts. This is evident when Piñeyro is read within the historical trajectory of the literature. His message is just as powerful, however. Marginality and invisibility were heavy burdens for Piñeyro to bear. His plight is mindful of the situation of Ralph Ellison's "invisible man," who affirms his existence as a "man of substance," "flesh and bone," with a "mind," but is not recognized for who he is.[7] Writing was Piñeyro's chosen form of resistance to alienation from self, others, and society. The body of work he left demonstrates that Richard Piñeyro was a master of his craft.

Conclusion

THE MOST RECENT U.S. STATE DEPARTMENT REPORT ON HUMAN rights in Uruguay, as reported in *El País,* offers the following assessment of blacks in that country:

> La comunidad negra, que constituye el 5.9 por ciento de la población total, enfrenta una discriminación social dado que los negros practicamente no tienen representación académica, política, burocrática ni en otros sectores de la sociedad porque carecen de los contactos necesarios para la entrada a esos grupos, afirma . . . El informe recordó también que la tasa de desempleo de los negros es 1.5 veces la de los blancos y ganan menos del 60 por ciento de los ingresos promedio que ellos.[1]

> [The black community, which makes up 5.9 percent of the total population, faces social discrimination given the fact that black people practically do not have academic, political or bureaucratic representation nor in other sectors of society because they lack the necessary contacts to enter those groups, the report affirms. The report pointed out also that the unemployment rate of blacks is 1.5 times higher than that of whites and they earn less than 60 percent of the median income of whites.]

The U.S. State Department made no recommendations regarding remedies to the racism experienced by Afro-Uruguayans. It is ironic that this report appeared during the period of Carnival, when black culture is most visible during the competitive phase of the "comparsas." Aside from this annual exploitation of black song and dance for export, they have not "overcome."

Afro-Uruguayans are caught in the double bind of trying to maintain a sense of ethnic identity while participating in the national cul-

151

ture as equals. On the one hand, there is the effort by officials to institutionalize Afro-Uruguayan rituals while organizations such as Mundo Afro continue to resist total absorption by the mainstream. The result is a tense social dynamic being played out in one of the few remaining enclaves of black culture in the Southern Cone.

The younger generation of Afro-Uruguayans is not immune from the pressures inherent in being "different" in that country. In his essay, "La política cultural de las Américas: El desalojo Afro-Uruguayo"/ "Cultural Politics of the Americas: The Afro-Uruguayan Eviction," Romero J. Rodríguez refers to a study of self-esteem among black youngsters conducted by Hector Florit, "Implicancias del racismo en el sistema educativo formal"/"Implications of Racism in the Formal Educational System" (1994), in which Florit states:

> En relación a la autovaloración personal, y en función de las observaciones del maestro, surge que 2 de cada 3 niños negros tienen una pobre autoestima o desvalorización de su persona.[2]

> [In relation to personal self-evaluation and as a result of observations by the teacher, it emerges that two of every three black children have poor self-esteem or devaluing of himself.]

The sense of inferiority, ingrained into the Afro-Uruguayan population at an early age, is difficult to overcome. Yet all Afro-Uruguayans have not passively accepted a situation as second-class citizens. Throughout their history, organizations and individuals have sought to emphasize positive cultural values and contributions.

Regarding the negative self-perception of Afro-Uruguayans, Rosa Luna has written:

> Permanentemente marcamos la diferencia hallando siempre más graves los defectos del negro. Los que por alguna circunstancia favorable lograron un estudio y una cultura no la utilizan en bien de la raza. Sólo pretenden compararse a los blancos y ganarse su aceptación, no el cariño de los suyos. Por eso reniegan sus raíces y tradiciones; y la envidia los carcome si uno menos culto logra superarlos en el afecto y reconocimiento de la gente. Cada tanto alzan su voz mencionando la esclavitud y el racismo. Sólo para mostrar que son diferentes y resaltar su verborragia. En los hechos poco hacen, y les produce asco si al cordón de la vereda un negro empina una botella o repica un tamboril. (66)

> [We note permanently the difference always finding more grievous the defects of black people. Those who through some favorable cir-

cumstance achieve education and culture do not use it for the good of the race. They only pretend to compare themselves with white people to win their acceptance and not the love of their own. For that reason they deny their roots and traditions; and envy eats them up if one less learned manages to supersede them in affection and recognition by the people. Every once in a while they raise their voice mentioning slavery and racism. Only to show they are different and to highlight their verbiage. Indeed they do little, and they are disgusted if out in the street a black man raises a bottle or beats a drum.]

The internalized self-hate and negation of black values among the more affluent Afro-Uruguayans have served to thwart progress historically. It is only through the consciousness-raising efforts and social actions of Mundo Afro, for instance, that a positive change in black self-perception and social responsibility is slowly occurring. Rosa Luna's perceptions are not distant from the goals of many aware Afro-Uruguayans: "Yo quiero para el futuro hombres inteligentes en mi raza, con idénticas posibilidades. Que hagan valer sus derechos, sin que esto signifique dejar de lado lo que nuestros ancestros nos legaron: el vino, el tamboril, el candombe" ["I wish for the future intelligent people in my race, with identical possibilities. Let them value their rights, without this meaning disregarding what our ancestors left us: wine, drum, candombe"] (66).

Afro-Uruguayan journalists, creative writers, performers, and social activists have been consistent throughout history in their collective call for an affirmation of black values and a reassessment of their place in the national history. Although many have predicted that Afro-Uruguayans will suffer the same fate as their Argentine counterparts, gone and forgotten, this is not likely to occur so long as the pockets of resistance remain and Blacks become empowered to write more of their own history.

The deaths in the 1990s of Alberto Britos, Manuel Villa, and Ruben Galloza in 2002 left a huge void in the advocacy of Afro-Uruguayan culture. For more than fifty years, Britos had labored in the black press from the early days with *Nuestra Raza* to *Bahía Hulan-Jack* in the present; Villa had established and maintained *Bahía Hulan-Jack* against all odds; and Galloza interpreted, in his paintings, Afro-Uruguayan popular culture better than anybody. Britos, Galloza, and Villa took with them irreplaceable knowledge of the Afro-Uruguayan cultural legacy. Ironically, the reliance upon Alberto Britos to tell their story, in writing, unchallenged, has left Afro-Uruguayans without a strong intellectual voice or presence.

In a study of periodicals and intellectuals that I authored, entitled *Afro-Argentine Discourse: Another Dimension of the Black Diaspora* (1996), some of the same issues inherent in the Afro-Uruguayan context were addressed and analyzed. I began the study with *La raza Africana* (1858), [*The African Race*] the first published Afro-Argentine periodical, and ended with the works of Tomás Platero, a contemporary poet and social activist. The literary trajectories as well as the assertion of an ethnic identity and the foregrounding of other aspects of culture were and are similar in these two countries of the Southern Cone. In Argentina, also, periodicals were fundamental in the construction of a black cultural identity. However, whereas in Argentina blacks who descended from the era of slavery have almost been totally absorbed into the majority culture, Afro-Uruguayans remain visible and some demand to be reckoned with on their own terms.

Notes

PREFACE

1. J. Jorge Klor de Alva, "The Postcolonialization of the (Latin) American Experience: A Reconsideration of 'Colonialism,' 'Postcolonialism,' and 'Mestizaje,'" in *After Colonialism: Imperial Histories and Postcolonial Displacements*, ed. Gyan Prakash (Princeton: Princeton University Press, 1995), 245. Afro-Uruguayans are hesitant to apply the term "hybridity" to their situation. Robert Young reminds us of "how influential the term 'hybridity' was in imperial and colonial discourse in negative accounts of the union of disparate races—accounts that implied that unless actively and persistently cultivated the hybrids would inevitably revert to their 'primitive' stock. Hybridity thus became, particularly at the turn of the century, part of a colonialist discourse on racism." Bill Ashcroft, Gareth Griffiths, and Helen Tiffin, *Key Concepts in Post-Colonial Studies* (New York: Routledge, 1998), 120.

2. Mario J. Valdés and Linda Hutcheon, *Rethinking Literary History—Comparatively*, ACLS Occasional Paper, no. 27, 1994, 2.

CHAPTER 1. PLACE AND DISPLACEMENT

1. Bill Ashcroft, Gareth Griffiths, and Helen Tiffin, *The Post-Colonial Studies Reader* (New York: Routledge, 1995), 391.

2. Luis Ferreira, *Los tambores del Candombe* (Montevideo: Colihue-Sepé Ediciones, 1997), 40. This information is based upon documentation provided by Lino Suárez Peña, Afro-Uruguayan historian, in *La raza negra en el Uruguay*, 19–20.

3. Gustavo Goldman, *¡Salve Baltasar!: La fiesta de reyes en el Barrio Sur de Montevideo* (Montevideo: Fondo Nacional de Música, 1997), 12–13.

4. *Revista Uruguay* 2, 20–21 (Septiembre-Octubre 1946): 5.

5. Luis Ferreira, *Los tambores del Candombe*, 77. A poignant poetic tribute is rendered to this site by don Alberto Britos in the unpublished poem "Mediomundo":

> Cayó el mediomundo
> cayó
> altivo y sin honores
> cayó.

Primero monumento
luego museo
al final, demolición;
refugio de artistas
pintores y tamborileros
africanos y carnavaleros.

Cayó el mediomundo
cayó
altivo y sin honores
cayó.

Conventillo de entrañas
anchas como el mar
cuna de tantos
cerquita del mar
hoy queda el recuerdo
de tu humano calor.

Cayó el mediomundo
cayó
altivo y sin honores
cayó.

Cayó para siempre
el "convento"
cayó para siempre
sin un repique
sin una fogata
sin un boro-cotó.

Cayó el mediomundo
cayó
altivo y sin honores
cayó.

Cayó el mediomundo
del viejo Palermo
sin un repique
sin un lagrimón
cayó el mediomundo
altivo y sin honores
CAYO PARA SIEMPRE
CAYO.

[Mediomundo fell
it fell
proud and without honors
it fell.

First a monument
then a museum
finally, demolition;
a refuge for artists
painters and drummers

Africans and carnivalgoers.

Mediomundo fell
it fell
proud and without honors
it fell.

A tenement with guts
wide as the sea
birthplace of so many
near the sea
today the memory remains
of its human warmth

Mediomundo fell
it fell
proud and without honors
it fell.

It fell forever
the "convent"
it fell forever
without a peal
without a spark
without a boro-cotó.

Mediomundo fell
it fell
proud and without honors
it fell.

Mediomundo fell
from old Palermo
without a peal
without a big tear
mediomundo fell
proud and without honors
IT FELL FOREVER
IT FELL.]

6. Romero J. Rodríguez, "El desalojo afro-uruguayo," paper presented at the University of Texas-Austin, 1996.

7. Redoblante (Nelson Domínguez), "El tambor abuelo convoca al ritual de la comparsería," *El País*, 5 February 1999, sec. 2, 1.

8. Alberto Britos Serrat, ed., *Antología de poetas negros uruguayos*, tomo 2, 2nd ed. (Montevideo: Ediciones Mundo Afro, 1997): 52.

9. Alberto Britos Serrat, ed., *Antología de poetas negros uruguayos*, (Montevideo: Ediciones Mundo Afro, 1990): 55–56.

10. *El País*, 31 January 1999, sec. 4, 2.

11. Martha Gularte, "Cuareim y Ansina," in *Antología de poetas negros uruguayos*, 2, 46.

12. Juan Julio Arrascaeta Jr., "Medio Mundo y Calle Ansina," in ibid., 54.

13. José Santos Carlos Barbosa, "Lavanderas del Medio Mundo," in ibid., 39.

14. Nelson Domínguez, *El País*, 9 February 1999, 18.

CHAPTER 2. PERIODICALS

1. Richard Jackson, *Black Writers in Latin America* (Albuquerque: University of New Mexico Press, 1979), 96.

2. Named after Salvador, Bahia-Brazil and a New York politician, the journal never deviated from its stated intention: "fundada por y para la propagación fundamental de la cultura del negro, difundirá los movimientos centrífugos de los negros estelares de la Humanidad y responde a los nombres ilustres—de tipo universal—que brevemente se hará la historia" [founded by and for the fundamental propagation of black culture, it will spread the centrifugal movements of brilliant blacks of Humanity and respond to illustrious names—universally—which soon will make history"]. No. 1, May 1958, 1. Regarding Hulan Jack, Philip Kasinith writes: "In 1940 he was elected to the New York State Assembly with Tammany support and in 1953 he was elected borough president of Manhattan. He thus became one of the highest ranking black officeholders in the nation and the only one not representing an overwhelmingly black constituency." *Caribbean New York: Black Immigrants and the Politics of Race* (Ithaca: Cornell University Press, 1992), 216.

3. "Hoy, como ayer," *Revista Uruguay*, 1, 1 (February 1945): 2.

4. "Una Ojeada Sobre Nuestra Sociedad," *La Conservación: Organo de la Sociedad de Color*, 1 (4 August 1872): 2.

5. Marcos Padín, "A la raza de color," *La Conservación*, 17 (November 1872): 3.

6. Editorial, *Nuestra Raza*, 1, 1 (10 March 1917): 1.

7. Editorial, *Rumbos*, 1 (25 August 1938): 1.

8. "De Nuevo en la Brecha," *La Vanguardia*, 1, 1 (15 January 1928): 1.

9. Editorial, *Acción*, 1, 1 (15 October 1934): 1.

10. María Esperanza Barrios, *La Verdad: Órgano de la Colectividad de Color*, 2, 44 (15 December 1912): 4.

11. Ventura Barrios, "Hasta aquí," *Nuestra Raza* 1, 30 (31 December 1917): 1.

12. "La Situación del momento y nuestra hoja," *La Verdad*, 3, 82 (31 July 1914): 1–2.

13. Editorial, *La Vanguardia*, 2, 29 (15 March 1929): 1.

14. "A los lectores," *Revista Uruguay*, 4, 43 (October 1948): 9.

15. Danilo Antón, "A nuestro abuelo negro," in *Ansina me llaman y Ansina yo soy* (Montevideo: Rosebud Ediciones, 1996), 11.

16. John A. Crow, *The Epic of Latin America* (Berkeley: University of California Press, 1980), 456.

17. Danilo Antón, *Uruguaypiri* (Montevideo: Rosebud Ediciones, 1994), 47. Antón explains: "Los descendientes de los Afro-Artiguistas permanecieron en Loma Campamento, siendo conocidos como los negros de 'Cambacua' (El agujero de los negros) y ellos se autodenominaron las 'Artigas Cué' (El pueblo de Artigas)." [The descendants of Artigas's black followers remained in Loma Compamento, being known as the blacks of 'Cambacua' (the hole of the blacks), and they called themselves the 'Artigas cue' (the people of Artigas)"], 48.

18. "Manifiesto a la Raza Negra," *Renovación* 1, 1 (31 July 1939): 2.

19. "Ansina," *Nuestra Raza*, 1, 4 (November 1933): 7.

20. "Reimpatriación de los restos de Ansina," *Nuestra Raza* 6, 63 (30 November 1938): 3.

21. "Cambá Cuá," *ABC Weekend* (Asunción), 31 May 1996, 5.

22. "Reimpatriación," *Nuestra Raza*, 6, 63 (30 November 1938): 3.

23. Daniel Hammerly Dupuy and Victor Hammerly Peverini, *Artigas en la poesía de América*, vol. 2 (Buenos Aires: Editorial Noel, 1951), 476.

24. Luisa Luisi, "Casi todos te olvidaron," in *Ansina me llaman y Ansina yo soy*, 5.

25. Isidoro Casas Pereyra, "Poema a mi abuelo negro," *Ansina*, 3, 3 (18 May 1941): 4.

26. José Roberto Suárez, "Es Así," *Nuestra Raza*, 8, 90 (28 February 1941): 5.

27. José Roberto Suárez, "Ansina," *Rumbo Cierto*, 1, 5 (1945): 1.

28. Pilar Barrios, "Ansina," *Acción* 3, 23 (25 August 1946): 1.

29. Cledia Núñez, "Evocación de Ansina," in *Antología de poetas negros uruguayos*, ed. Alberto Britos (Montevideo: Colección Mundo Afro, 1990), 59–60.

30. Romero Rodríguez, "Carta del Director," *Mundo Afro* 1, 1 (August 1988): 3.

31. Afro-Uruguayan periodicals with their initial dates of publication (Montevideo, unless otherwise indicated):

> *La Conservación: Órgano de la Sociedad de Color*, 1, no. 1, 4 August 1872.
> *La Propaganda: Órgano Defensor de los Intereses de esta Colectividad*, 1, no. 1, 3 September 1893.
> *La Verdad*, 1, no. 1, 15 September 1911.
> *Nuestra Raza* (San Carlos), 1, no. 1, 10 March 1917.
> *La Vanguardia: Órgano Defensor de los Intereses de la Raza Negra*, 1, no. 1, 15 January 1928.
> *Nuestra Raza: de la Raza, por la Razy y para la Raza*, 1, no. 1, 25 August 1933.
> *Acción* (Melo), 1, no. 1, 15 October de 1934.
> *PAN: Órgano del Partido Autóctono Negro*, 1, no. 1, 15 April 1937.
> *Rumbos* (Rocha): *Periódico Independiente de la Raza de Color*, 1, no. 1, 25 August 1938.
> *Ansina: Órgano del Comité Pro-Homenaje a Don Manuel Antonio Ledesma*, 1, no. 1, 18 May 1939.
> *Renovación*, 1, no. 1, 31 July 1939.
> *Democracia* (Rocha), 1, no. 1, 26 May 1942.
> *Rumbo Cierto*, 1, no. 1, November 1944.
> *Revista Uruguay*, 1, no. 1, February 1945.
> *Bahia Hulan Jack*, no. 1, May 1958.
> *Mundo Afro*, 1, no. 1, August 1988.

CHAPTER 3. AFRO-URUGUAYAN DRUM CULTURE

1. Tomás Olivera Chirimini and Antonio Varese, *Memorias del tamboril* (Montevideo: Editorial Latina 1996), 55. The authors then pose the question, "¿Es algo genético o aprendido?" This rhetorical question misses the entire point of Repique's argument, which is that there is a marked difference between "playing" a drum and "beating" one.

2. Luis Ferreira, *Los tambores del Candombe* (Montevideo: Ediciones Colihue-Sepé, 1997), 98.

3. Josaphat B. Kubayanda, *The Poet's Africa: Africanness in the Poetry of Nicolás Guillén and Aimé Césaire* (New York: Greenwood Press, 1990), 89.

4. Carlos Cardozo Ferreira, "Del sentir de mi raza," *Partido Autóctono Negro* 1, 5 (15 August 1937): 4.

5. José Roberto Suárez, "Tambor," *Antología de poetas negros uruguayos*, ed. Alberto Britos (Montevideo: Colección Mundo Afro, 1990), 54.

6. Martha Gularte, "El tamborilero," *Antología de poetas negros uruguayos*, ed. Alberto Britos (Montevideo: Colección Mundo Afro, 1997), 47.

7. Miguel Angel Duarte López, "Tamboril," *Antología de poetas negros uruguayos* (1997), 80.

8. Juan Julio Arrascaeta Jr., "Tamborilero," *Antología de poetas negros uruguayos* (1997), 49.

9. Abril Trigo, "Candombe and the Reterritorialization of Culture," *Callaloo* 16, 3 (1993): 716. The best discussion of Candombe as folklore is Paulo de Carvalho Neto, "The Candombe, A Dramatic Dance from Afro-Uruguayan Folklore," *Ethnomusicology* 6, 3 (1962): 164–74.

10. Isidoro de María, *Montevideo antiguo*, vol. 2 (1888), 2nd ed. (Montevideo: Biblioteca Artigas, 1957), 280.

11. Lauro Ayestarán, *Las músicas primitivas en el Uruguay* (Montevideo: Arca, 1997), 93–94. The "Canto Patriótico de los Negros Celebrando la Ley de Libertad de Vientres y a la Constitución" was published in *El Parnaso Oriental o Guirnalda Poética* (1835), 229–32.

12. Rubén Carámbula, *El Candombe* (Buenos Aires: Ediciones del Sol, 1995), 13.

13. Luis Ferreira, *Los tambores del Candombe* (Montevideo: Ediciones Colihue-Sepé, 1997), 36.

14. Oscar Montaño, *Umkhonto: Historia del aporte negro-africano en la formación del Uruguay* (Montevideo: Rosebud Ediciones, 1997), 98.

15. Magdalena Arrarte and Susana Nin, "Una pareja de negros viejos," *El País*, sec. 3, 14 February 1999, p. 5.

16. Alberto Britos, *Antología de poetas negros uruguayos* (Montevideo: Ediciones Mundo Afro, 1990), 53.

17. José Roberto Suárez, "Candombe," *Revista Uruguay* 2, 22 (1946): 7.

18. *Antología de poetas negros uruguayos*, 2nd ed. (Montevideo: Ediciones Mundo Afro, 1997), 66.

19. Paulo de Carvalho, *El carnaval de Montevideo: Folklore, historia, sociología* (Sevilla: Universidad de Sevilla, 1967), 173.

20. Ferreira, *Los tambores del Candombe*, 76.

21. "La Comisión de Fiestas y la Sociedad de Color," *La Verdad*, 2, 15 (5 February 1911): 1.

22. Iris M. Cabral, "Carnaval o ¿qué?" *Nuestra Raza* 2, 20 (23 March 1935), 7.

23. Mario L. Montero, "Exaltación Lubola," *Nuestra Raza* 6, 65 (30 January 1939): 7.

24. "Carnaval," *Nuestra Raza* 3, 77 (30 January 1940), 1.

25. Guillermo Rosas, "Las cartas sobre la mesa," *Mundo Afro* 1, 2, 2n época (22 February 1998): 5.

26. Rosa Luna, *Rosa Luna: sin tanga y sin tongo* (Montevideo: Ediciones Del Taller, 1988), 17.

27. Nelson Domínguez, "Las Llamadas," *El Pais*, 7 February 1999, 2nd sec., 6.

Chapter 4. Resistance and Identity

1. Jonathan Culler, *Literary Theory: A Very Short Introduction* (New York: Oxford University Press 1997), 110.

2. Homi K. Bhabha, *The Location of Culture* (New York: Routledge, 1994), 46.

3. Alberto Britos Serrat, *Antología de poetas negros uruguayos* (Montevideo: Colección Mundo Afro, 1990): Tomo II, 1995: Segunda Edición, 1997.

4. Martha Cobb, *Harlem, Haiti and Havana* (Washington, D.C.: Three Continents Press, 1979), 53.

5. Timoteo Olivera, "A los hombres de color," *La Conservación* 8 (22 September 1872): 1.

6. Carlos Cardozo Ferreira, "Negro en la noche," *Nuestra Raza* 3, 31 (23 February 1936): 6.

7. Carlos Cardozo Ferreira, "Invitación a negrita," *Nuestra Raza* 7, 75 (30 November 1939): 9.

8. Juan Julio Arrascaeta, "La negrita," *Revista Uruguay* 3, 26 (March 1947): 6.

9. Ibid.

10. Pilar Barrios, "Raza negra," *Revista Uruguay* 2, 19 (August 1946): 13.

11. Britos Serrat, *Antología de poetas negros uruguayos*, 12.

12. Alberto Britos Serrat, *Antología de poetas negros uruguayos*, tomo 2 (Montevideo: Ediciones Mundo Afro, 1996–7): 12.

13. Teresa Porzencanski and Beatriz Santos, eds., *Historias de vidas: Negros en el Uruguay* (Montevideo: Ediciones Populares para América Latina, 1994), 48–49.

14. Alberto Britos, review of *Pregón de Marimorena, Nuestra Raza* 12, 153 (May 1946): 9.

15. Iris Virginia Salas, "Mi corazón," *Acción*, 2nd época, 1, 11 (25 April 1944): 5.

16. "Virginia Brindis de Salas, *Acción*, 2nd época, 2, 23 (25 August 1946): 10.

17. Virginia Brindis de Salas, *Cien cárceles de amor* (Montevideo: Compañía Impresora, 1949), 32.

18. Cledia Núñez de Altamiranda, "Canto negro" (Poema en 3 cantos) in *Antología de poetas negros uruguayos*, ed. Alberto Britos (Montevideo: Colección Mundo Afro, 1990), 57–59.

19. Cristina Rodríguez Cabral, "Montevideo" in *La del espejo y yo* (Montevideo: 1989).

20. Cristina Rodríguez Cabral, "Memoria y Resistencia" in *PALARA* 4 (fall 2000): 104–5.

CHAPTER 5. JORGE EMILIO CARDOSO

1. "Nuestro teatro," *Renovación* 1, 1 (31 July 1939): 3. Zenona Suárez Peña appears in the periodical literature as the leading Afro-Uruguayan actress of the 1930s and 1940s.

2. "Nuestro teatro," *Renovación*, 1, 3 (25 September 1939): 3.

3. *Nuestra Raza* 19, 107 (30 July 1942): 2.

4. *Nuestra Raza* 3, 25 (24 August 1935): 12.

5. Roberto Cisnero, "Candombe," *Nuestra Raza*, 10, 112 (December 1942): 17.

6. "César A. Techera: su actuación artística," *Rumbos*, 2 época, 1, 2 (September 1948): 3.

7. "Una hora de Amena Charla con Isabelino José Gares," *Nuestra Raza*, 2 época, 21 (20 April 1935): 2-3. Juanamaría Cordones-Cook comments briefly on the trajectory of Gares in *Teatro Negro Uruguayo*, 19-20, but does not analyze any of his works.

8. *Nuestra Raza* 4, 13 (1937): 4.

9. "'José Isabelino Gares'"—autodidacta, . . . sentía un gran amor por su raza, tan digna y tan poco respetada en sus derechos. Y como contribución a su mejoramiento, leal desinteresadamente expuso sus anhelos en la prensa negra y valientemente llevó el problema al teatro . . . joven aún, el autor de *El Camino de la Redención* muere el 20 de julio de 1940" ["'José Isabelino Gares'"—self-taught, . . . felt a great love for his race, so dignified and so little respected in its rights. And as a contribution to its betterment, loyally he espoused his concerns in the black press and valiantly carried the problem to the theater . . . still young, the author of *The Road to Redemption* died on 20 July 1940"]. *Nuestra Raza* 11, 131 (July 1944): 5.

10. José Isabelino Gares, "Los Escritores y la Raza Negra," *Acción* 1, 9 (15 February 1935): 2. "Banguelas," "Congas," and "Magi" are names of African ethnic groups and "nations" in Uruguay. According to Alberto Britos, the Banguelas/Benguela are of Angolan origin; Congas refer to Africans from the Congo and blacks in general; while the Magi are from Dahomey. *Glosarios de Afronegrismos uruguayos* (Montevideo: Ediciones Mundo Afro-El Galeón, 1999), 28, 53, 86.

11. Juanamaría Cordones-Cook, "Cuando los negros hacían teatro," *Paula* (14 February 1997): 15.

12. Advertisement, *La Vanguardia* 1, 24 (31 December 1928): 3.

13. Isidoro Casas Pereyra, "José I. Gares, Poeta y Dramaturgo de Color," *Rumbos* 3, 25 (25 August 1940): 16.

14. José Isabelino Gares, *El camino de la redención: Ensayo de Comedia Racial en Dos Actos* (Montevideo: Talleres Gráficos, 1931), 1. I thank Sonia Gares, daughter of the playwright, who sent me a copy of this text for use in this study.

15. "CIAPEN y su verdadera misión," *Rumbos* 2nd época, 1, 3 (July 1949): 8.

16. Juanamaría Cordones-Cook, "Interview with Tomás Olivera Chirimini," in *¿Teatro negro uruguayo? texto y contexto del teatro afro-uruguayo de Andrés Castillo*, (Montevideo: Ediciones el Galeón, 2000), 39. The same point is made by "Carlos" who states: "El Teatro Negro Independiente era propiedad material y espiritual del Dr. Merino, cuya obra anda por ahí. Lo vi un poco patriarcal y yo soy renuente a esas actitudes, entonces nunca me acerqué a él" ["The Independent Black Theatre was material and spiritual property of Dr. Merino, whose work is out there. I saw that he was a bit patriarchal, and I resist those attitudes, therefore I never approached him"]. *Historia de vidas: Negros en el Uruguay*, 47.

17. Rafael Murillo Selva Rendón, *Loubavagu o el otro lado lejano* (Tegucigalpa, Honduras: Litografía López, 1998). This "crónica teatral musicalizada"/"musicalized theatrical chronicle" in Garífuna and Spanish is characterized as a work that "captura nuestro subconsciente nacional desde el lenguaje mítico de la música y la danza: palabra en movimiento, mensaje que cautiva sin forzosamente decimos los episodios del presente o del pasado" ["captures our national subconscious from the mythic language of music and dance: word in motion, message which captures without force we say episodes from the present to the past"] (Julio Escoto). The works of Jorge Emilio Cardoso are destined to evolve into interpretations as profound.

18. Letter to author from Jorge Emilio Cardoso, 18 August 1992.

19. Jorge Emilio Cardoso, *Los horizontes de Calunga* (Montevideo: AEBU, 1992), 36.

20. Keir Elam, *The Semiotics of Theatre and Drama* (New York: Methuen, 1980), 93.

21. Lauro Marauda, "De los gastados pretileo, ya no saluda el palomo macho," *La República* (1 November 1995), 3.

22. Jorge E. Cardoso, *El desalojo de la calle de los negros* (Montevideo: np, 1997), 6. This play was first published in the *Afro-Hispanic Review* 15, 2 (1996). It was subsequently self-published by Cardoso in 1997. *Los condenados* by Jorge Emilio Cardoso was also published in the *Afro-Hispanic Review*, 20, 2 (fall 2001): 40-48.

23. Bill Ashcroft, Gareth Griffiths, and Helen Tiffin, *The Empire Writes Back: Theory and Practice in Post-Colonial Literatures* (New York: Routledge, 1989), 28.

CHAPTER 6. RICHARD PIÑEYRO

1. Luis Bravo, "Recuerdo de Richard Piñeyro: una poesía esencial," *El País Cultural*, no. 541 (17 March 2000): 10.

2. Richard Piñeyro, "El día de la noche," in *Prosa, poesía y algo más* (Montevideo: PENAL de Libertad, 1974), n.p.

3. Richard Piñeyro, "A Emilio," in *Quiero tener una muchacha que se llame Beba* (Montevideo: Ediciones de Uno, 1982), 7.

4. Richard Piñeyro, "Carta a Laura," *Cartas a la vida* (Montevideo: Ediciones de Uno, 1985), 15.

5. Richard Piñeyro, "Confession of R.P.," *El otoño y mis cosas* (Montevideo: Ediciones de Uno, 1992), 28.

6. Richard Piñeyro, Carlos Brandy, introduction, *Palabra antigua* (Montevideo: Vintén Editor, 1999), 5.

7. Ralph Ellison, *Invisible Man* (New York: Random House, 1994), 3.

CONCLUSION

1. *El País* (27 February 1999: 10. Three years earlier, in a survey conducted by *El Observador*, the Uruguayan daily, the investigators concluded: "Los uruguayos no consideran que actúen en forma discriminatoria pero admiten la segregación—por distintos motivos—es una realidad en el país." "Iguales, pero no tantos." ["Uruguayans don't believe they act in a discriminatory manner but they admit that segregation—for different reasons—is a reality in the country." "Equals, but not too much."], *El Observador—Fin de semana*, 30 de marzo, 1996, p. 1.

2. Romero Jorge Rodríguez, "La política cultural de las Américas: El desalojo Afro-Uruguayo," paper presented at the University of Texas-Austin, 1996, 12.

Bibliography

Antón, Danilo. *Uruguaypirí.* Montevideo: Rosebud Ediciones, 1994.

Antón, Danilo, and Armando Miraldi. *Ansina me llaman y Ansina yo soy.* Montevideo: Rosebud Ediciones, 1996.

Arias, Jorge. "Los grandes problemas están en la calle." *La República* (9 November 1995): 43.

———. "Los más destacados." *La República* (17 December 1995): 44.

Ashcroft, Bill et al. *The Empire Writes Back: Theory and Practice in Post-Colonial Literatures.* New York: Routledge, 1989.

———. *Key Concepts in Post-Colonial Studies.* New York: Routledge, 1998.

———. *The Post-Colonial Studies Reader.* New York: Routledge, 1995.

Ayestarán, Lauro. *Las músicas primitivas en el Uruguay.* Montevideo: Arca, 1997.

Bhabha, Homi. *The Location of Culture.* New York: Routledge, 1994.

Bravo, Luis. "Recuerdo de Richard Piñeyro: una poesía esencial." *El País Cultural* 541 (17 March 2000): 10.

Britos, Alberto. *Antología de poetas negros uruguayos.* Montevideo: Ediciones Mundo Afro, 1990.

———. *Antología de poetas negros uruguayos.* Tomo II. Montevideo: Ediciones Mundo Afro, 1996. 2nd ed. 1997.

———. *Glosario de afronegrismos uruguayos.* Montevideo: Mundo Afro—El Galeón, 1999.

Bula Píriz, R. "Letras Afro: Jorge Emilio Cardoso," *La República* (1 March 1997): 13.

Canzani, Agustín. "Racismo Cordial," *El Observador* (30 March 1996): 2-3.

Capi, Mirta Amarilla. *La música en el Uruguay.* Montevideo: Graphisur, 1983.

Carámbula, Rubén. *El Candombe.* Buenos Aires: Ediciones del Sol, 1995.

Cardoso, Jorge Emilio. *El desalojo de la calle de los negros.* Montevideo: np, 1997.

———. *Los horizontes de Calunga.* Montevideo: AEBU, 1992.

———. *Los condenados. Afro-Hispanic Review* 20, no. 2 (fall 2001): 40–48.

Carvalho-Neto, Paulo de. "The Candombe, A Dramatic Dance from Afro-Uruguayan Folklore." *Ethnomusicology* 6, no. 3 (September 1962): 164–74.

————. *El Carnaval de Montevideo: Folklore, Historia, Sociología.* Sevilla: Universidad de Sevilla, 1967.

————. *Estudios Afros: Brasil, Paraguay, Uruguay, Ecuador.* Caracas: Universidad Central de Venezuela, 1971.

————. *El negro uruguayo.* Quito: Editorial Universitaria, 1965.

Casas Pereyra, Isidoro. "José I. Gares, Poeta y Dramaturgo de Color." *Rumbos* 3, no. 25 (25 August 1940): 16.

Chagas, Jorge. *La soledad del General: la novela de Artigas.* Montevideo: La Gotera, 2001.

Chirimini, Tomás Olivera, and Juan Antonio Varese. *Los candombes de reyes: Las Llamadas.* Montevideo: Ediciones el Galeón, 2000.

————. *Memorias del tamboril.* Montevideo: Editorial Latina, 1996.

Cobb, Martha. *Harlem, Haiti and Havana.* Washington, D.C.: Three Continents Press, 1979.

Cordones-Cook, Juanamaría. *¿Teatro negro uruguayo?: Texto y contexto del teatro afrouruguayo de Andrés Castillo.* Montevideo: Editorial Graffiti, 1996.

Crow, John A. *The Epic of Latin America.* Berkeley: University of California Press, 1980.

Culler, Jonathan. *Literary Theory: A Very Short Introduction.* New York: Oxford University Press, 1997.

da Luz, Alejandrina. "Uruguay," *No Longer Invisible: Afro-Latin Americans Today,* ed. Minority Rights Group, 332–44. London: Minority Rights Publication, 1995.

de María, Isidoro. *Montevideo Antiguo.* Vol. 2, 2nd ed. 1888. Reprint, Montevideo: Biblioteca Artigas, 1957.

"Desalojo de la calle de los negros," *La República* (27 December 1998): 11.

Diagnóstico socioeconómico y cultural de la mujer afrouruguaya. Montevideo: Ediciones Mundo Afro, 1998.

Diggs, Irene. "The Negro in the Viceroyalty of the Río de la Plata," *Journal of Negro History* 36, no. 2 (1951): 281–301.

Diverso, Gustavo, and Enrique Filqueiras, comp. *Montevideo en Carnaval: Genios y Figuras.* Montevideo: Editorial Monte Sexto, 1992.

E. I. "Teatro en el Barrio Reus." *Búsqueda* (3 November 1995): 50.

Elam, Keir. *The Semiotics of Theatre and Drama.* New York: Methuen, 1980.

Ellison, Ralph. *Invisible Man.* 1952. Reprint, New York: Random House, 1994.

Ferreira, Luis. *Los tambores del Candombe.* Montevideo: Ediciones Colihue-Sepé, 1997.

Frijerio, Alejandro. "Estudios sobre los afrouruguayos: Una revisión crítica." *Cuadernos del Instituto Nacional de Antropología y Pensamiento Latinoamericano* 16 (1995): 411–22.

————. "'Oye mi tambor': La imagen del negro en las comparsas lubolas del Carnaval de Montevideo." *Cuadernos del Instituto Nacional de Antropología y Pensamiento Latinoamericano* 17 (1996/97): 1–27.

Gares, Isabelino José. *El camino de la redención.* Montevideo: Talleres Gráficos, 1931.

————. "Noche de Reyes." *La Vanguardia* 2, no. 25 (15 January 1929): 4.

Gascue, Alvaro. *Partido Autóctono Negro—un intento de organización política de la raza negra en el Uruguay.* Montevideo: np, 1980.

Goldman, Gustavo. *¡Salve Baltasar!: La Fiesta de Reyes en el Barrio Sur de Montevideo.* Montevideo: Universidad de la República, 1997.

Graceras, Ulises. *Informe preliminar sobre la situación de la comunidad negra en el Uruguay.* Montevideo: Dirección General de Extension Universitaria, 1980.

Hammerly Dupuy, Daniel, and Victor Hammerly Peverini. *Artigas en la poesía de América,* vol. 2. Buenos Aires: Editorial Noel, 1951.

Jackson, Richard L. *Black Writers in Latin America.* Albuquerque: University of New Mexico Press, 1979.

Kasinith, Philip. *Caribbean New York: Black Immigrants and the Politics of Race.* Ithaca: Cornell University Press, 1992.

Kordon, Bernardo. *Candombe: contribución al estudio de la raza negra en el Río de la Plata.* Buenes Aires: Editorial Continente, 1938.

Kubayanda, Josaphat B. *The Poet's Africa: Africanness in the Poetry of Nicolás Guillén and Aimé Césaire.* New York: Greenwood Press, 1990.

Lewis, Marvin. *Afro-Argentine Discourse: Another Dimension of the Black Diaspora.* Columbia: University of Missouri Press, 1996.

———. *Afro-Hispanic Poetry, 1940–1980: From Slavery to "Negritud" in South American Verse.* Columbia: University of Missouri Press, 1983.

Luna, Rosa. "El Apartheid Uruguayo." *El Día* (8 October 1989): 22.

———. *Sin tanga y sin tongo.* Montevideo: Ediciones Del Taller, 1988.

Merino, Francisco M. *El negro en la sociedad montevideana.* Montevideo: Ediciones de la Banda Oriental, 1982.

Montaño, Oscar D. *Umkhonto: Historia del aporte negro-africano en la formación del Uruguay.* Montevideo: Rosebud Ediciones, 1997.

———. *Yeninyanya: Historia de los Afrouruguayos.* Montevideo: Ediciones Mundo Afro, 2001.

"Nuestro Teatro." *La Vanguardia* 1, no. 23, (15 December 1928): 2.

Ortiz Oderigo, Nestor. *Calunga: croquis del Candombe.* Buenos Aires: Universidad de Buenos Aires, 1969.

Páez Villaró, Carlos. *Las Llamadas: viaje de medio siglo a través de la tamborería.* Montevideo: Artes Gráficos Integradas, 2000.

Parkash, Gyan. *After Colonialism: Imperial Histories and Postcolonial Displacements.* Princeton: Princeton University Press, 1995.

Pelfort, Jorge. *Abolición de la esclavitud en el Uruguay.* Montevideo: Ediciones de la Plaza, 1996.

Pereda Valdés, Ildefonso. *El negro en el Uruguay: pasado y presente.* Montevideo Revista del Instituto Histórico y Geográfico del Uruguay, XXV, 1965.

———. *El negro rioplatense y otros ensayos.* Montevideo: Claudio García & Cia., 1937.

Picotti, Dina C., *La presencia africana en nuestra identidad.* Buenos Aires: Ediciones del Sol, 1998.

Pierri, Ettore. *Una mujer llamada Rosa Luna.* Montevideo: Ediciones La República, 1994.

Piñeyro, Richard. *Cartas a la vida.* Montevideo: Ediciones de Uno, 1985.

———. *El otoño y mis cosas.* Montevideo: Ediciones de Uno, 1992.

———. *Palabra antigua*. Montevideo: Vintén Editor, 1999.

———. *Quiero tener una muchacha que se llame Beba*. Montevideo: Ediciones de Uno, 1982.

Porzecanski, Teresa, and Beatriz Santos, comp. *Historias de vidas: negros en el Uruguay*. Montevideo: Ediciones Populares para América Latina, 1994.

Rama, Carlos M. *Los afro-uruguayos*. Montevideo: El Siglo Ilustrado, 1967.

Ramírez, Beatriz. "Uruguay: integración de la comunidad negra," *Afroamericanos: buscando raíces, afirmando identidad* 4 (1995): 30–31.

Ruegger, Gustavo Adolfo. "No sólo candombe," *El País* (17 October 1995): 11.

Santos, Beatriz. "El tipo de discriminación que hay en el Uruguay es sutil y solapado. Es en silencio." *El Día* (8 October 1989): 22.

———. *La herencia cultural africana en las Américas*. Montevideo: Ediciones Populares para América Latina, 1998.

Santos, Beatriz, and Nené Lorriaga. *Africa en el Río de la Plata: el racismo*. Buenos Aires: Editorial Amerindia, 1995.

Selva Rendón, Rafael Murillo. *Loubavagu o el otro lado*. Tegucigalpa: Litografía López, 1998.

Suárez Peña, Lino. *La raza negra en el Uruguay: novela histórica de su paso por la esclavitud*. Montevideo: np, 1933.

Trigo, Abril. "Candombe and the Reterritorialization of Culture," *Callaloo* 16, no. 3 (1993): 716–28.

Valdés, Mario J., and Linda Hutcheon. *Rethinking Literary History—Comparatively*. ACLS Occasional Papers, No. 27, 1994.

Vidart, Daniel. *El espíritu del Carnaval*. Montevideo: Editorial Graffiti, 1997.

Whitten, Norman E., and Arlene Torres, eds. *Blackness in Latin America and the Caribbean*. 2 vols. Bloomington: Indiana University Press, 1998.

Young, Caroll Mills. "Virginia Brindis de Salas vs. Julio Guadalupe: A Question of Authorship," *Afro-Hispanic Review* 12, no. 2 (1993): 26–30.

———. "The New Voices of Afro-Uruguay," *Afro-Hispanic Review* 14, no. 1 (1995): 58–64.

Index

169